CliffsNotes™

Investing in Mutual Funds for Canadians

by John Craig and Juliette Fairley

IN THIS BOOK

- ■ Understand the different kinds of mutual funds
- ■ Learn how experienced investors evaluate funds
- ■ Make sense of mutual fund terms and jargon
- ■ Pick a fund that matches your financial goals
- ■ Reinforce what you learn with CliffsNotes Review
- ■ Find more mutual fund information in CliffsNotes Resource Centre and online at www.cliffsnotes.com

CDG Books Canada, Inc.

CDG
BOOKS
C A N A D A

About the Authors

John Craig is a Toronto-based freelance writer whose work has appeared nationally in publications such as *Maclean's*, *The Globe and Mail*, *Investment Executive*, and *IE:Money*.

Juliette Fairley is a personal finance writer whose work has appeared in *USA Today*, *The New York Times*, *Investor's Business Daily*, and other publications. Her first book, *Money Talks: Black Finance Experts Talk to You about Money*, was published in 1998 by John Wiley & Sons.

Publisher's Acknowledgements
Editorial

Senior Project Editor: Mary Goodwin
Acquisitions Editors: Joan Whitman, Mark Butler
Copy Editor: Liba Berry
Technical Reviewer: Charm Darby, CFP, PFP

Production

Project Coordinator: Donna Brown
Text Production: Kyle Gell Art & Design
Proofreader: Martha Wilson
Indexer: Wendy Thomas

CliffsNotes Investing in Mutual Funds for Canadians
Published by
CDG Books Canada, Inc.
99 Yorkville Avenue
Suite 400
Toronto, ON M5R 3K5
www.cdgbooks.com (CDG Books Canada Web site)
www.cliffsnotes.com (CliffsNotes Web site)
www.idgbooks.com (IDG Books Worldwide Web site)

Canadian Cataloguing in Publication Data
Craig, John
    Investing in mutual funds for Canadians

(CliffsNotes)
Includes index.
ISBN 1-894413-13-X

1. Mutual Funds — Canada. I. Fairley, Juliette, 1966–. II. Title. III. Series.
HG5154.5.C72 2000   332.63'27   C99-932654-6

Printed in Canada.

1 2 3 4 5 TRI 04 03 02 01 00

Distributed in Canada by CDG Books Canada, Inc.
For general information on CDG Books, including all IDG Books Worldwide publications, please call our distribution centre: HarperCollins Canada at **1-800-387-0117**. For reseller information, including discounts and premium sales, please call our Sales department at **1-877-963-8830**.
This book is available at special discounts for bulk purchases by your group or organization for resale, premiums, fundraising and seminars. For details, please contact our Special Sales department at **1-877-963-8830** or Email: spmarkets@cdgbooks.com.
For authorization to photocopy items for corporate, personal, or educational use, please contact Cancopy, the Canadian Copyright Licensing Agency, One Yonge Street, Suite 1900, Toronto, ON M5E 1E5; Tel: **416-868-1620**; Fax: **416-868-1621**; www.cancopy.com

Table of Contents

INTRODUCTION

You're looking at this book because you're interested in investing in mutual funds. That's good! You can see as you read the chapters that we're definite believers in mutual funds. For millions of people, they represent the easiest, most affordable, most diversified, and most profitable way to build an investment nest egg. Whether your financial objective is a secure retirement, a university education for your children, a new home, a business of your own, or some combination of these and other goals, mutual funds can help you reach your objectives.

In the past two decades, millions of investors in Canada, along with many more in the United States and abroad, have discovered the advantages of mutual funds. As a result, the mutual fund industry enjoys the status of a booming business. In Canada alone, there are now over 1,700 different mutual funds available, with over $360 billion in assets under management. (Keep in mind that as recently as 1981, assets under management in Canada totalled a mere $3.5 billion — this unprecedented growth has made the mutual fund industry the fastest-growing sector of the Canadian financial services industry.)

And this enormous pool of money is not being squandered on get-rich-quick schemes or some kind of paper-shuffling mumbo-jumbo designed to make a few Bay Street big shots wealthy. As you discover in this book, the money invested in mutual funds goes to buy stocks and bonds issued by businesses and government agencies around the world.

Knowledge about putting your money to work for you is especially important today. You and your family are beginning to take greater responsibility for your own financial well-being. In fact, you don't really have a choice. Here are some of the reasons:

- The days of lifetime job security are gone. Today's businesses pride themselves on remaining "lean and mean," eliminating jobs whenever necessary to keep profits high. You must take responsibility for your financial safety and not rely on a job that may evaporate tomorrow.

- The days of the guaranteed company pension are gone. You may be self-employed, hold temporary positions, or change careers frequently, so you can't expect to retire from a company that has provisions to support you in old age. Even if you do stay at one firm for a long time, you may be expected to fund your own retirement.

- The Canada Pension Plan (CPP) is on shaky ground. You may not be able to count on government benefits kicking in at the same age and income level that they do today.

- The cost of a university education or a home in a good neighbourhood is higher than ever before. Without an aggressive program of saving and investing, you may not be able to afford the components of the "good life."

- People are living longer than ever. That's good news, of course, but increased longevity also means that you need to plan for a retirement that lasts 20 to 40 years rather than 10 to 15.

This book, designed in the tradition of CliffsNotes, can help you get started investing in mutual funds, with simple, straightforward, basic advice in an easy-to-understand form. You won't learn *all* there is to know about mutual funds — that could take a lifetime. But you *will* learn all the facts you need to begin investing in mutual funds for profit — and even a little fun.

Why Do You Need This Book?

Can you answer yes to any of these questions?

- Do you need to learn about mutual funds fast?

■ Don't have time to read 500 pages on mutual funds?

■ Are you trying to save for a university education, a home, or a new car?

■ Do you want to retire in comfort?

If so, then CliffsNotes *Investing in Mutual Funds for Canadians* is for you!

How to Use This Book

This book is yours to use in whatever ways suit you best. You can either read the book from cover to cover or skip around from chapter to chapter. If you want quick and easy access to a particular topic, you can

■ Use the index in the back of the book to find what you're looking for.

■ Flip through the book looking for your topic in the running heads.

■ Look for your topic in the Table of Contents in the front of the book.

■ Look at the In This Chapter list at the beginning of each chapter.

■ Look for additional information in the Resource Centre or test your knowledge in the Review section, both sections at the back of the book.

■ Or, flip through the book until you find what you're looking for — we organized the book in a logical, task-oriented way.

Also, to locate important information quickly, you can look for icons strategically placed next to text. Here is a description of the icons you can expect to find throughout this book:

This icon introduces a fact, concept, or connection that's too important to forget.

This icon highlights a suggestion or idea that can save you time and energy, make you money, or make your life easier.

This icon introduces an important caution about a potentially dangerous situation or a mistake that's easy to make. If you ignore the information presented here, you're in jeopardy of losing time, money, or peace of mind. Don't worry — in each case, we also tell you what to do to avoid the danger.

Don't Miss Our Web Site

Keep up with the changing world of investing by visiting the CliffsNotes Web site at www.cliffsnotes.com. Here's what you find:

■ Interactive tools that are fun and informative

■ Links to interesting Web sites

■ Additional resources to help you continue your learning

At www.cliffsnotes.com, you can even register for a new feature called *CliffsNotes Daily*, which offers you newsletters on a variety of topics, delivered right to your e-mail inbox each business day.

If you haven't yet discovered the Internet and are wondering how to get online, pick up Getting on the Internet, new from CliffsNotes. You'll learn just what you need to make your online connection quickly and easily. See you at www.cliffsnotes.com!

CHAPTER 1

BEFORE YOU INVEST IN MUTUAL FUNDS

IN THIS CHAPTER

- Analyzing your financial situation
- Setting financial goals
- Determining your appetite for risk
- Finding the money to begin investing
- Looking forward to feathering your nest over time

Before you invest in mutual funds — or any other investment — you need to ask yourself a few key questions. Most importantly, you must know where you are going before you start the journey. One key to investing wisely is knowing both your financial goals and your investment horizon. Are you investing for retirement 25 years down the road, to finance a child's education in 15 years, or to buy a home in 5? Or are you investing for a short-term goal, like a new car or a great vacation next summer? The answers to these questions greatly influence the kinds of investments that are right for your consideration — and financial outlay.

You also need to understand your own money personality — your willingness to take on risk and uncertainty when you invest, and how comfortable you are with markets that may change the value of your investments every day.

Finally, you need to figure out the source of your investment dollars: Where will you get the money to begin investing? Several avenues are worthy of exploring, even when budgets are tight: trimming needless expenses, reducing debt, and participating in an automatic investing plan at work. The sooner you start investing, the quicker the power of *compounding* — money growing over time — can work for you. We explain the concept of componding in detail later in this chapter.

Setting Your Financial Goals

When you start thinking about investing in mutual funds, you need to first determine your financial goals. Why are you interested in investing? What do you hope to do with the profits you may make? Although mutual funds are well known for their potential in retirement planning, investors use them to address a wide variety of financial goals.

You can think of financial goals as *short-term, long-term,* or a combination of the two.

Short-term goals

Short-term goals are those material targets you set your sights on hitting within one to three years from today. Typical short-term goals include

■ A vacation next summer

■ A new car to replace the old one you're driving now

■ Upgraded appliances for your kitchen

All these goals have two things in common. First, they cost more money than most people expect in a single paycheque. Second, the amount of money needed to achieve any of these goals is manageable enough to enable most people with a steady income to accumulate the cash within one to three years — provided they save and invest.

When saving for a goal that is three years away or less, a practical investment option is a particular type of mutual fund called a *money market fund*. Money you invest in a money market fund grows slowly but steadily, with little fluctuation in value. You can read more about money market funds in Chapter 5.

Long-term goals

Long-term goals are those for which most people save and invest for longer than 10 years. Most people have two main long-term goals:

- A full-time university education for one or more children, including tuition and living expenses

- A secure, comfortable, and enjoyable retirement

Long-term goals involve investing your money and leaving it in your investment until you need it, 10 years or more in the future. Patience and persistence are key to long-term investments, in at least three ways:

- You need to invest steadily, a few dollars every month, if you want your investment to grow.

- You have to leave the money alone — don't withdraw cash every time you're tempted by a sale at the local mall or attracted by the sleek lines of a new-model car.

- You must accept the fact that most investments rise and fall in value. Resist the urge to panic when your investment takes a dip. The setback is probably only temporary.

The tendency of investments to rise and fall in value is called *volatility*. Maybe you've heard about stock market crashes or other sudden drops in investment values; perhaps you've seen pictures of frightened investors screaming into their phones or even jumping out of windows in despair.

When volatility is extreme, anxiety is a normal reaction. The benefit of long-term investing is that market fluctuations don't matter as much. As a long-term investor, you have time for your investments to rebound — as they usually do. Because a long-term investor has time to weather the ups and downs of a changing market, he or she can invest in mutual funds such as equity funds with more aggressive investment objectives. Read more about these types of funds in Chapter 4.

Although the stock market always rises and falls in the short term, the market's long-haul investment history shows that no other kind of investment grows so steadily or so much. Thus, long-term money generally belongs in the stock market, and equity (stock) funds are a great way to go.

Figure 1-1: A place for you to list your short- and long-term goals.

Short-term goals	$$$	Time frame
☐ _____	_____	_____
☐ _____	_____	_____
☐ _____	_____	_____
☐ _____	_____	_____

Long-term goals	$$$	Time frame
☐ _____	_____	_____
☐ _____	_____	_____
☐ _____	_____	_____
☐ _____	_____	_____

A combination of goals

What if, like most people, you have both short-term and long-term goals? You probably want to save for retirement *and* for a new car. How do these dual goals affect your investment strategy?

The answer is simple: Divide the money you have to invest into two or more streams, and invest in more than one kind of mutual fund. Each month, set aside a certain amount of money for short-term goals, and invest those dollars in a fund that is low-risk and not very volatile — even though the growth of your money may not be spectacular.

At the same time, set aside another sum for long-term saving, and invest that money in more aggressive equity funds, whose upside potential — that is, opportunity for truly impressive growth — is greater. This set of investments may rise or fall, month by month, but over time these funds are likely to outperform your short-term money — if you're patient enough to let it happen.

How much of your investment money should go toward short-term investing, and how much toward long-term? That depends on several factors, especially the relative importance of various financial goals to you and your age (which affects the length of time until you retire or send children to university). For many people, a 50/50 split is a reasonable starting point, to be adjusted as you see fit over time.

Dividing your investment money into two or more kinds of investments with different characteristics is known as *diversification*. Think of the basic law of diversification as "Don't put all your eggs in one basket." You reduce risk when you divide your money among different investments; even if one investment goes down in value, the other is likely to go up, balancing loss with profit and helping you come out ahead in the end.

We deal with diversification in Chapter 3. As you'll discover, avoiding having all your money tied up in any single investment is one of the basic principles of smart investing — and one of the main advantages you derive from any mutual fund investment.

Understanding Your Money Personality

In addition to determining your financial goals, you need to assess your personal relationship to money — specifically, your *risk tolerance*.

Some people are comfortable with the idea of investing their money in more aggressive — and more volatile — investments. They have the patience — and the psychological stamina — to stay calm as the value of their investments rises and falls, confident that they'll win out in the end.

Others can't stand this kind of uncertainty. They want to know exactly what their investments will be worth one year, two years, and ten years from now, and they don't want to be bothered with tracking the ups and downs of the market. Where you fall on this spectrum is your risk tolerance, your ability to live comfortably with a degree of financial uncertainty.

Which kind of investor are you? Does even the slightest fluctuation in your portfolio make you anxious? If so, you're probably a conservative investor. Can you imagine yourself sleeping soundly at night while knowing that your investments may be changing marginally in value? Then you're probably a moderate investor. Are you excited by the idea of investing as a kind of game and willing to take on substantially higher risk in order to gain higher returns? Then you may be classified as an aggressive investor. Determining your investor profile is vital to determining what investment choices are right for you.

If you're not sure about your own risk tolerance level and investor profile — as is true of many new investors — try this approach. Divide your investment money into two batches. Put one batch, perhaps three quarters of your money, into lower-risk investments. Put the rest into more aggressive, growth-oriented funds. (If you're starting from scratch, expect to take a little time to accumulate enough money to divide into two batches.) Then watch how these investments perform over the next five years.

Depending on how well you do with your "risk money," you may decide to gradually increase that investment, shift it to other types of funds, or reduce it. As you monitor your investments and make these kinds of decisions, your sense of your investor profile becomes clearer. You learn exactly what degree of risk you're comfortable with, and you develop an instinct for putting together an investment plan that's both profitable and psychologically acceptable to you.

Finding the Money to Invest

Finding money to invest in mutual funds requires the discipline of *not* spending and sticking to a budget. You need a bit of willpower and real determination to make it happen. If you decide to take $100 to $500 a month out of your salary to invest, you can find ways to trim the fat.

Here are some ways to reduce your spending without suffering undue hardship:

- Cutting back on going out to eat
- Avoiding daily trips for pricey coffees, soft drinks, and snacks
- Quitting smoking
- Renting movies to watch at home instead of going to the local theatre
- Keeping your aging-but-still-running car a year or two longer

Paying yourself first

Make saving and investing a priority. One way to do this without feeling financially deprived is to "pay yourself first."

That is, when you get your weekly or biweekly paycheque, *before* paying your usual bills — rent or mortgage, utilities, credit cards — set aside a regular amount for investing.

Put the predetermined sum — whether it's $100, $500, or even more — in a special savings account or write a cheque directly to the mutual fund of your choice. By allocating this money first, before you start spending on other things, you can more easily resist the temptation to skip a week or a month here and there along the investing trail. Furthermore, you may find that you hardly miss the extra money; you'll quickly adjust your spending habits to live on a little less each month, reinforced by the pleasure of watching your investment account grow.

Ask your employer about setting up a direct deduction — with the approval of Revenue Canada — from your paycheque to your registered retirement savings plan (for more on RRSPs, see Chapter 9). By using *source deduction,* you can reduce your taxable income upfront and get the benefit of a tax refund now, when you need it, instead of a year later at tax time. This strategy can also help increase your cash flow. In addition, depending on the profit-sharing plan available through your employer, you may be able to participate in a program that allows your employer to match your contribution. For example, for every dollar you invest, your employer will match with 50 cents. If your company offers such a plan, sign up for it immediately and go for the maximum percentage contribution allowed under their policies — for example, 6 percent of your gross income.

Trimming your credit card debt

The best way to improve your personal financial situation and to free up money for investing is by reducing your debt — especially costly credit card debt. In these days of easy credit, most people find their mailboxes stuffed daily with credit card offers from banks and other companies. It's temptingly easy to accept the offers, run up a balance with purchases, and then switch to yet another card.

The unwary person who owns and uses several credit cards can find himself carrying a total debt equal to half or more of his yearly income — an uncomfortable, costly, and dangerous way of life.

If you take the following steps to reduce the debt drain on your finances, you'll soon see your investment fund growing:

- Pay off credit card balances as soon as you can. At interest rates of 17 percent, 18 percent, or even higher, these are among the most expensive loans offered anywhere. The longer you take to repay them, the more each purchase costs.

- Start paying your total credit card balance each month rather than the minimum amount. This will force you to begin living on your current income instead of mortgaging your future for present purchases.

- If you own a home, consider consolidating and paying off your credit card balances with a home equity loan as the interest rates are usually lower. However, be careful — if you can't use the interest cost of the loan as a deduction, it may not be worth your time.

Putting Time to Work for You

Try to start investing regularly as soon as you can. Invested money grows by *compounding* — that is, the profits you earn on the money you invest generate additional profits, and these in turn generate more profits, for as long as you let your investment grow.

Compounding is a remarkably powerful wealth-building process that can turn relatively modest amounts of money into a fortune — provided you give the investment time to work.

Table 1-1 illustrates how compounding can work for you. The table assumes that you set aside $100 at the start of each month for investing purposes. Go down the table to the year that shows how long you expect to let your investment money grow. Then read across the table to see how much money you can expect to accumulate at various rates of return.

Table 1-1: How Compounding Works for You

Growth of a $100/month investment at various rates of return, with compounding.

			Rate of Return		
Year	4%	6%	8%	10%	12%
1	$1,230	$1,240	$1,250	$1,270	$1,280
2	2,500	2,560	2,610	2,670	2,720
3	3,830	3,950	4,080	4,210	4,350
4	5,210	5,440	5,670	5,920	6,180
5	6,650	7,010	7,400	7,810	8,250
10	14,770	16,470	18,420	20,660	23,230
15	24,690	29,230	34,830	41,790	50,460
20	36,800	46,440	59,290	76,570	99,910
25	51,580	69,650	95,740	133,790	189,760
30	69,640	100,950	150,030	227,930	352,990

If you set aside $100 a month, after 12 months you save $100 × 12 = $1,200. However, as the table shows, if this invested money earned a 10% rate of return, it would be worth $1,270 at the end of the first year. With compounding, the investment would grow faster the second year, reaching a value of $2,670 — fully $270 more than the amount you actually invested. And by the end of the tenth year, the same account would have grown to $20,660, which is $8,660 more than the amount you actually invested.

When the time frame extends far into the future — 25 to 30 years, or even longer — the power of compounding becomes truly awesome. As you can see, the same $100 per month investment has the potential to grow, after 30 years, to over $227,000. Naturally, if you manage to save two or three times more per month, your accumulated total would be two or three times greater.

CHAPTER 2

LEARNING ABOUT MUTUAL FUNDS

IN THIS CHAPTER

- Defining mutual funds
- Making money from owning a mutual fund
- Comparing closed-end and open-end funds

Mutual funds are a very popular means of investing money. A mutual fund pools money received from individual investors like you — often in modest amounts — to create a large investment fund. A professional fund manager with detailed knowledge of investing then puts this money to work for you. As the money grows over time, so does the value of your investment.

The money in mutual funds is usually invested either in stocks or bonds. *Stocks* represent shares in the ownership of companies. When you own stocks, you share in the profits the companies enjoy, and when the value of the companies grows, so does the value of your stocks.

Bonds, on the other hand, represent money that has been borrowed by a company or a government agency. When the loan is repaid, the owner of the bond gets the money back with interest. When you invest in a *mutual fund,* your money goes with the money of many other people to buy stocks or bonds. As the mutual fund that owns the stocks or bonds profits from these investments, so do you.

What Is a Mutual Fund?

A mutual fund is an investment vehicle that pools the money of many investors to buy a large number of investments. By pooling small amounts of money invested by thousands of individuals, a mutual fund can invest in dozens of different stocks, bonds, and other securities. When you buy shares in the fund, you become a part owner of all those investments, and as those investments grow, so will your money.

When you buy a share in a mutual fund, you are participating in the performance of all the investments selected by the manager of the fund. Most individuals don't have the resources to invest in a wide range of stocks, bonds, or other investment vehicles, nor do they have the money to hire a professional money manager to choose investments for them (see Figure 2-1).

Figure 2-1: Mutual fund investments can cover a broad range of possibilities.

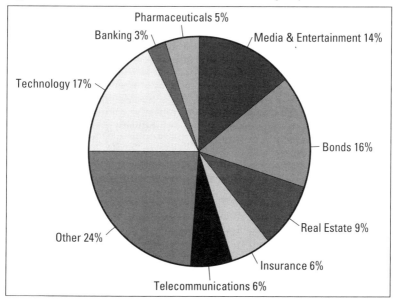

In order to understand how mutual funds work, you need to understand the difference between mutual funds and the stocks and bonds that are owned by a mutual fund.

A share of stock represents part ownership of a company. When you own a share of Bombardier, the Royal Bank of Canada, or Nortel Networks, you own a (tiny) portion of that company. If the company's sales and profits increase, you benefit: You're likely to receive *dividends,* which are payments of a portion of a company's profits to shareholders. Plus, the value of your stock probably increases as the company prospers.

By contrast, a bond is like an IOU. A bond represents a loan of money to the managers of a business or a government agency; they promise to pay you back, with interest, over a specified period of time. You can buy and sell bonds on the open market (usually with the help of a financial professional called a broker). When you buy a bond, you are purchasing the promise of repayment with interest. Like shares of stock, bonds may rise and fall in value.

Bonds usually change in value based on changes in interest rates: In general, when interest rates rise, bonds fall in value, and vice versa (see Figure 2-2).

A mutual fund is a collection of individual stocks, bonds, and other types of securities that are generally of interest only to financial specialists. The mutual fund manager selects the stocks and bonds based on the investment objectives of the particular fund and on the manager's judgment as to which investments are likely to be most profitable — these investments can range from Canadian common stocks to mortgages to treasury bills. (In later chapters, we explain how you can determine the objectives and style of a particular fund and whether that fund is a good choice for you.) In general, if the manager selects wisely, investors in the mutual fund benefit; if the manager's choices are poor, the investors suffer.

Figure 2-2: As interest rates rise, bond values fall.

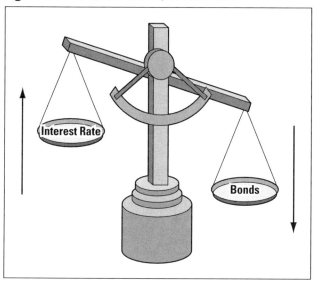

Thus, the main difference between a mutual fund and individual stocks and bonds is that the person who invests in a mutual fund owns units in an entire portfolio of stock or bond investments, managed by a knowledgeable financial professional. It's like handing your investment money to an expert and saying, "Here — you pick some good investments for me, and send me the profits."

The sale and trading of mutual funds, stocks, and bonds is regulated by provincial securities commissions that protect investors from fraud and theft. However, the value of your investment in a mutual fund is not guaranteed by the securities commissions or any other government institution.

Having said that, the only real way to lose money in a mutual fund investment is to sell the fund in a down market — otherwise, any drop means you're just experiencing market price fluctuation. Like any investment, you have to accept a degree of risk, and the mutual fund risk scale ranges from minuscule to very high. If you want to minimize risk, you can focus your investment in a vehicle such as a money market fund — no money market fund sold in Canada has ever lost money for investors. (See Chapter 5 for more on money market funds.)

How You Profit from a Mutual Fund

When you own units in a mutual fund, you stand to profit in three different ways:

■ Through any increase in the value of the stocks and/or bonds owned by the fund (the *net asset value*)

■ Through any dividends paid to the fund by the companies issuing the stocks and/or bonds

■ Through any profits earned by the fund when they buy and sell stocks or bonds (*capital gains*)

Net asset value

The value of the stocks and/or bonds owned by a mutual fund is usually stated in terms of net asset value (NAV). As the value of the securities in a fund moves up and down, the NAV (and the purchase price) of your fund changes accordingly.

Net asset value is expressed as the value of all the securities (stocks and/or bonds) in the mutual fund portfolio divided by the number of shares of the mutual fund owned by investors. The resulting net asset value per share is the price at which shares in the fund can be bought or sold.

For example, if a mutual fund owned stocks with a total value of $1 billion and investors owned 100 million shares of the fund, the net asset value per share would be $1 billion ÷ 100 million = $10. Thus, it would cost an investor $10 to buy a single share in the fund, and an investor who sold a share in the fund would receive $10 for it.

Because the values of stocks and bonds change from day to day, the NAV of any mutual fund also fluctuates on a daily basis. As the NAV of a fund you own rises, so does the value of your shares. When you decide to sell those shares, you receive more money than you paid for them, reflecting the higher value. (Of course, the NAV of a fund may sometimes fall.)

If you're interested, you can find the current NAV of many mutual funds listed in the business pages of your daily newspaper. Figure 2-3 contains a sample mutual fund listing, from the *National Post* for October 9, 1999. Notice how the paper provides the following kinds of information:

- **Fund Family:** This is the company that owns and manages the specific mutual funds. Some companies, like AGF (shown in Figure 2-3), operate dozens of funds with various investment objectives and styles.

- **Fund Name:** Shown in abbreviated form, this is the name of the specific mutual fund. In this listing, AGF's 20/20 "Aggr Gth" (second from the top) stands for Aggressive Growth, whereas "Cdn Res" (a few lines down) translates to Canadian Resources and "India" names a fund that specializes in stocks of companies based in that country.

- **NAVPS:** The net asset value per share, as described earlier in this section, as of the end of the previous business day. In this sample listing, AGF's 20/20 Aggressive Growth fund had a NAV of $33.05 per share.

- **Daily $ and % Return:** Yesterday's change in value of NAV from the previous day. In the listing shown, the NAV of AGF's 20/20 Aggressive Growth fund had fallen by 0.9 percent from the previous day, lowering its NAVPS by $0.30. If you're an investor in the fund, you don't want to see a downward trend continue indefinitely.

- **52W High and Low:** This is the highest and lowest NAVPS reached by the fund in the past 52 weeks. In the past year, AGF's 20/20 Aggressive Growth Fund has been as high as $34.44 and as low as $14.02.

- **Weekly NAVPS:** The highest and lowest NAVPS the fund reached in the past week. In this sample listing, AGF's 20/20 Aggressive Growth fund reached a high of $33.39 and a low of $31.92. This section also provides both the dollar and percentage change of the fund over the previous week. (You can learn much more about how to judge investment performance later in this book, especially in Chapter 7.)

Figure 2-3: Typical listing of mutual fund data in a daily newspaper.

MUTUAL FUNDS 10.08.99

Figures supplied by Fundata Canada Inc.

52W high	52W low	Fund	Spec.	Fri. NAVPS. $chg	%chg	Wkly NAVPS high	low	cls	$chg	%chg
AGF Group of Funds										
9.17	5.59	20/20 Aggr Gbl	FD	0.00	0.00	9.03	8.77	9.03	0.36	4.15
34.44	14.02	20/20 Aggr Gth	FD	-0.30	-0.90	33.39	31.92	.33.05	2.03	6.54
15.83	11.32	20/20 Cdn Res	*FD	-0.07	-0.47	15.23	14.68	14.68	-0.50	-3.29
4.20	2.38	20/20 Emerg Mkt	FD	0.02	0.51	3.98	3.89	3.98	0.08	2.05
3.64	1.92	20/20 India	FD	0.06	1.68	3.64	3.38	3.64	0.24	7.06
4.72	2.82	20/20 Latin Am	FD	0.01	0.27	3.75	3.63	3.75	0.10	2.74
3.41	1.78	20/20 Mgd Fut	*FD	-0.03	-0.90	3.37	3.32	3.32	0.07	2.15
6.93	5.43	20/20 RSP Ag Eq	*ZFD	0.03	0.52	5.84	5.78	5.83	-0.02	-0.34
5.85	4.61	20/20 RSP Ag Sm	*FD	0.06	1.19	5.11	5.01	5.11	0.09	1.79
37.23	23.66	AGF Amer Grth	FD	0.54	1.56	35.07	34.14	35.07	1.68	5.03
24.82	20.75	AGF Amer TAA	FD	0.24	1.04	23.37	22.92	23.37	0.56	2.46
12.21	7.63	AGF Asian Grth	FD	-0.05	-0.46	10.87	10.54	10.82	0.26	2.46
5.68	4.30	AGF Cda Class	FD	0.04	0.72	5.57	5.48	5.57	0.13	2.39
5.76	5.32	AGF Cdn Bond	*FD	0.00	0.00	5.36	5.32	5.32	-0.02	-0.37
23.55	17.44	AGF Cdn Stock	*FD	0.17	0.75	22.90	22.54	22.90	0.55	2.46

How to read the mutual fund tables

Mutual fund rate of return figures appear in the Financial Post Mutual Funds Monthly Report, which runs the third Saturday of each month.

1. 52-week high/low: Highest and lowest price reached in the previous 52 weeks
2. Fund: name
3. Specifics: footnotes: ✝ – denotes segregated fund Y– delayed NAVPS or yield U– US$ ✱ – RRSP eligible (funds without * may generally be held in RRSPs as foreign property) X – trading ex-dividend Z – not available to general public N – no load fund F – front-end load or fee D – deferred declining redemption fee based on original capital invested R – deferred declining redemption fee based on market value FD – For D at buyer's option FR – For R at buyer's option B – both front- and back-end fee ... –
data not available
Friday NAVPS data:
4. Dollar change: from previous day

1	2	3	4 5	6 7 8 9 10
52W 52W	Fund		Fri. NAVPS	Wkly NAVPS
high low		Spec.	$chg %chg	high low cls $chg %chg
9.51 6.63	Global Equity	FR	0.10 1.31	7.75 7.31 7.75 0.76 10.87

5. % Change: from previous day
Friday NAVPS data:
6. High on week
7. Low on week
8. Close on week
9. % Change from previous week
Money Market Funds
Data for money market funds and segregated

money market funds reflect current yields, not NAVPS. For example, under "dollar change" the figures would indicate the change in a fund's current yield in terms of percentage points. Pricing and yield data supplied by Fundata Canada Inc. is for information purposes only. Confirmation of price should be obtained from the fund sponsor.

The newspaper listings also include footnotes of various kinds, indicated by lowercase letters next to the fund names. Visually scan the newspaper page for an explanation of these cryptic letters. By looking up the explanations, you can learn, for example, that the "FD" next to AGF's 20/20 Aggressive Growth fund means the buyer has a choice between a front-end load fee (upfront sales commission) or a deferred sales charge. This is a worthwhile piece of information if you're considering buying shares in this fund. (We explain these and other mutual fund fees in Chapter 6.)

Dividends

Dividends are a portion of the profits earned by a company, which the company may distribute to their stockholders.

Not all companies pay dividends. Young, quick-growing companies may choose to reinvest all their profits in further company growth, spending the money to hire new employees, buy new technology, or develop new business ideas. However, older, more-established companies often pay regular dividends — usually four times a year — to their shareholders, calculated on the basis of so many cents per share owned. For example, if a company decides to pay its shareholders a dividend of 50 cents per share, an individual who owns 200 shares of that company's stock will receive a cheque for $100.

When a mutual fund owns stock, the fund receives the dividends and distributes them to investors, usually in the form of additional fund shares. Thus, the value of your mutual fund investment grows when the stocks owned by the fund pay dividends.

Capital gains

The mutual fund manager buys and sells stocks and bonds continually, in response both to changing market conditions and to the flow of money into or out of the fund. When the manager sells a stock or bond at a higher price than he paid for it, the difference is a kind of profit known as a capital gain. As with dividends, the capital gains received by a mutual fund are distributed to owners of the fund, usually in the form of additional fund shares.

Warning

At the end of each year, the mutual fund provides a tax receipt that distinguishes income from the fund as interest, dividends, or capital gains. For funds held in tax-advantaged plans such as registered retirement savings plans (RRSPs) and registered retirement income funds (RRIFs), the income is not taxed, but for funds held outside a registered plan, the income must be reported. (Read Chapter 9 for a detailed explanation of how to be tax-savvy when it comes to the growth of your mutual fund investments.)

Closed-End Funds versus Open-End Funds

The most popular kind of mutual fund is known as an *open-end fund*. (In fact, unless it's otherwise stated, you can assume that any mutual fund you hear or read about is an open-end fund.) An open-end fund continuously issues new shares and redeems old shares on demand.

When such a fund is popular, money flows in to the fund manager from investors who are eager to own shares. The manager then invests this new money in additional stocks and/or bonds. New shares in the fund are constantly being created.

By contrast, *closed-end funds* issue a fixed number of shares. After investors buy these shares, no more money can enter the fund. If you want to sell shares that you own, you don't sell them to the fund management firm, as with an open-end fund. Instead, the shares trade on an exchange, much like the trading of shares in the stock of individual companies. Thus, the price of a share in a closed-end fund is set by supply and demand: If investors are eager to buy the shares, the price rises; if not, the price falls.

Like an open-end fund, a closed-end fund has a net asset value, computed by dividing the total value of the fund's portfolio holdings by the number of shares. However, the shares of a closed-end fund may sell at a *premium* to the NAV (that is, for more than the NAV) or at a *discount* to the NAV (that is, for less than the NAV).

For instance, if a particular closed-end fund has an NAV of, say, $15 per share, the actual price at which the shares trade may be higher (say, $18 per share) or lower (say, $11 per share).

Of course, you're better off buying shares of a closed-end fund at a discount rather than at a premium. In fact, experts generally advise investors to buy closed-end fund shares *only* when they're available at an attractive discount.

A mutual fund company may decide to offer a closed-end fund rather than an open-end fund for several reasons. The main consideration: a desire to *avoid* having too much money to invest.

With a closed-end fund, the fund manager knows how much money he must handle; he doesn't continually get new money to invest, as may be the case with an open-end fund. In some investment markets, closed-end may be a better way of doing business.

For example, an emerging market (that is, a new or relatively undeveloped business region, such as South America or Eastern Europe) may have only a limited number of good companies in which to invest. The manager of a fund specializing in such a market may worry about taking in more money than he can invest wisely. A closed-end fund solves this problem.

For the average investor, open-end funds are a better choice than closed-end funds. Newspapers and financial magazines, and Internet sites such as the Fund Library, cover open-end funds more extensively, which makes it easier to track them. They are more liquid than closed-end funds — that is, easier and more convenient to buy and sell. And their prices are less volatile; upward and downward movement is slower and more predictable.

Some sophisticated investors are especially interested in closed-end funds, but these are probably not the best starting point for the individual who is new to mutual funds.

CHAPTER 3

RECOGNIZING THE PROS AND CONS OF MUTUAL FUNDS

IN THIS CHAPTER

- Recognizing the advantages of investing in mutual funds
- Understanding diversification, liquidity, and shareholder services
- Recognizing the disadvantages of investing in mutual funds
- Looking at the risks

No one investment is right for everyone. Like any other investment, mutual funds have both advantages and disadvantages. The disadvantages are real, and you need to understand the potential drawbacks before you invest. Nonetheless, for millions of people, mutual funds are the most convenient, diversified, and profitable way to invest.

Advantages of Investing in Mutual Funds

Mutual funds invest in the same kinds of stocks and bonds that individual investors can (and do) buy — so why employ a middleman (the fund manager)? What benefits do you enjoy from investing through a mutual fund rather than purchasing directly?

Putting your money to work in mutual funds provides distinct advantages over other forms of investments. If, after you weigh the pros and cons, you decide to take the plunge, you're likely to come up with your own additions to the list of benefits.

Diversification

Diversification involves spreading your money around among several different kinds of investments in order to reduce the risk of concentrating in a single security (see Figure 3-1). When your investments are diversified, you don't take a major hit if any one investment performs poorly. Thus, the savvy investor avoids concentrating all her investments in the stock of a single company, or even a single industry.

Figure 3-1: Reducing your risk by diversifying.

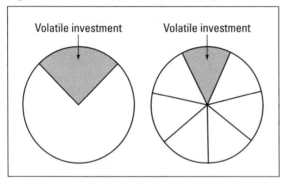

You may be lucky enough to work for a company that helps you invest or awards you *stock options* — the opportunity to buy the company's stock at a special, often discounted, price. Either way, you enjoy a great reward for being an employee.

But be careful — employees sometimes end up investing almost their entire savings in the stock of the company they work for. All is well as long as the company is flourishing. But if the industry suffers a downturn, or if your own company happens to go bankrupt, you may find that your investment is suddenly worth little or nothing.

Mutual funds also allow you to diversify your investments at a relatively low cost. Because of transaction costs (the fees charged when you buy or sell stock), you can waste time and money buying one or two shares of stock in a dozen different companies, which may be all that an investor with a couple of thousand dollars can afford. But the same investor can easily afford to invest in one or more mutual funds. Buying mutual fund shares makes you a part owner of many different types of stocks (or bonds), giving you the benefits of diversification at a fraction of the cost.

Remember

By definition, any mutual fund offers some degree of diversification because every fund invests in many different stocks or bonds. But some funds are more diversified than others. For example, *sector funds,* which concentrate on investing in a single industry, are less diversified than most other stock funds. When economic trends favour that industry, the corresponding sector fund profits.

For example, during the late 1990s, sector funds that concentrate on the stock of Internet companies and other high-tech businesses have done very well. If and when high-tech industry flounders, however, the technology funds will, too. Thus, keeping all your money in one such fund would be a risky strategy.

Low entry cost

You can get started in mutual fund investing with relatively little money — a benefit when finances are tight, but you're mentally ready to roll with an investment experience.

You can start investing in most mutual funds with as little as $500 for an initial investment. In fact, many mutual fund companies will even allow you to get started for as little as $25 to $50, as long as you agree to some sort of automatic monthly deduction plan from your chequing account.

Professional management

Mutual funds hire smart investment experts to manage your money, and they have access to extensive research into companies, economic conditions, and market trends. Most people would have a hard time keeping track of a large number of investments in many different businesses; staying on top of that financial activity is part of the daily routine for the research staff of a mutual fund.

Liquidity

Liquidity refers to the ease with which you can buy or sell an investment. Buying or selling a particular stock or bond, especially one held by relatively few people, may be difficult. If you need cash in an emergency, this obstacle to turning your investment into legal tender can cause inconvenience and may cost you money. By contrast, mutual fund shares can be cashed in quickly at any time by redeeming them with the managing company, usually at little or no cost.

Shareholder services

Many mutual fund companies offer a range of useful, sometimes valuable services to their customers. These may include

- Cheque-writing privileges
- Ability to invest, withdraw, or move money via mail, telephone, or the Internet
- Automatic investment via payroll deduction
- Record-keeping for filing your income tax return
- Access to research reports about companies, funds, and economic trends

A fund's prospectus tells you more about such services.

Disadvantages of Investing in Mutual Funds

Although mutual funds are tremendously varied, flexible, and convenient, they have disadvantages that you need to consider before investing.

Risks involving fund management

These days, mutual funds are among your wiser investment options. Diversification, professional management, and the watchful eye of provincial securities commissions (see an online list at www.cba.ca/eng/links_gov.htm or the provincial government pages in your local phonebook) and other regulatory bodies continue to help ensure that mutual funds stay that way. Nonetheless, investing in mutual funds carries various kinds of risk that can impact your financial planning.

One risk that's inherent in the nature of mutual funds is the fact that you, the investor, have no control over what's being purchased for the portfolio. You are putting your money — and your investment fate — in the hands of the fund manager, which is why you need to study the track record of the fund company and the individual manager before you invest.

Making sure that you're giving your money to a reliable financial partner is important to your wallet and your peace of mind. (We explain how to make sure you're selecting capable mutual fund managers in Chapters 7 and 8.)

Another unpredictable challenge may arise when a fund's "star" manager retires or changes jobs, leaving the fund without his expertise or brilliance. For example, Peter Lynch was one of the most successful and famous mutual fund managers in the world for many years. Under his guidance, the Fidelity Magellan Fund grew into the largest mutual fund anywhere, with over $72 billion (U.S.) in assets. Millions of investors poured money into Magellan, attracted largely by Lynch's reputation and prestige. Since Lynch's retirement in 1990, however, Magellan has performed with far less success, despite the strong performance of the stock market overall.

Warning

Past performance is no guarantee for future performance. If you're a fund investor, follow the financial news. Be aware when changes in the management of your funds occur. You may want to consider switching funds when the manager responsible for your fund's track record departs the scene.

Risk involving changes in the market

Even with expert management, however, the risk involved in mutual fund investing does not disappear. Sometimes, the stock or bond market as a whole may be in decline, and even smart investors are unable to make a profit. Such hard times are referred to as *bear markets.*

The opposite of a bear market is a time when the markets are steadily rising — *bull market.* Pessimistic investors are sometimes referred to as *bears,* while optimists are *bulls.* Now you understand the livestock references that you often hear scattered throughout financial news reports!

If you're a long-term investor, bear markets may not be a problem. You can probably wait until the market rebounds before selling your shares. A short-term investor, however, may get stuck with losses. Although you can't avoid risk altogether, you can choose money market mutual funds or other investments that don't tend to fluctuate dramatically, as we note in Chapter 1.

Unclear investment approach

Sometimes funds are managed in ways that contradict the image presented in advertising or promotion. A fund that is touted as a conservative fund — one that selects investments so as to minimize risk and volatility — may be managed in an aggressive manner, putting money into highly volatile small-company (small cap) stocks, for example.

A fund that calls itself a stock fund may actually keep a sizable portion of its investment money in cash or in short-term government bonds, which are considered equivalent to cash; thus, it may miss out on some of the gains enjoyed during a strong period for the stock market.

Instead of relying solely on advertising, press accounts, or the advice of a broker, always ask for a *prospectus* before investing in a fund. This is a legal document approved by a securities commission that discloses all pertinent information about the fund. Compare what you read in the prospectus with the sales pitch presented in ads or by a broker. If you feel there's a contradiction between them, don't hesitate to ask about it. (Chapter 7 contains more information about how to digest all the details in a prospectus, including the real clues to a fund's character.)

Lack of insurance for fund investments

Unlike investments such as term deposits or guaranteed investment certificates (GICs), your investment in a mutual fund is not insured by the Canada Deposit Insurance Corporation (CDIC) or any other government agency. Therefore, when the fund invests in securities that rise and fall in value, you have the possibility of losing your initial investment.

Tax inefficiency

Another disadvantage to mutual funds is that stock funds (also called *equity* funds) are not very "tax-efficient." Here's how this inefficiency plays out in your overall investment picture: When you own individual stocks, you decide when to buy and sell them.

When you sell a stock that has increased in price, you receive a type of profit known as a *capital gain*. At the end of the year, you must pay taxes to Revenue Canada on all the capital gains you enjoyed during that year. But with mutual funds, the schedule of stock purchases and sales is up to the fund manager — you don't have control of the timing.

Fortunately, there are funds managed specifically to minimize tax inefficiency. (We explain how this works in Chapter 9.)

Many stock investors carefully regulate their sales of stock so that they incur capital gains when the additional money is less burdensome to their tax situation. For example, a stock investor might choose to realize her capital gains during a year when her salary from work is smaller, thereby reducing her overall tax rate.

Mutual fund investing, however, means that you may receive capital gains distributions from the fund at any time. Of course, you end up paying taxes on these at the end of the year, unless your mutual funds are held within a tax-advantaged plan such as an RRSP or RRIF. (Tax-advantaged plans are also fully explained in Chapter 9.)

At tax time, mutual fund firms send out either a T3 or T5 tax receipt to their mutual fund investors. The document details taxable earnings. Don't fail to report this income on your return; the fund company is also reporting it to the Revenue Canada, which will check for discrepancies.

If you are in a high tax bracket — that is, if your overall income is large enough to make your combined federal and provincial tax rate burdensome — and if you have a significant amount of money to invest in the stock market (say, $25,000 or more), you *may* want to consider investing in individual stocks rather than mutual funds so that you can better control the tax effects of your investments.

We tell you more about the tax implications of mutual fund investing in Chapter 9.

Uncertainty about redemption price

When you own an individual stock, you can choose to sell it at any time during the trading day (that is, while the stock market is in operation), and you will get the price that's current at the moment you sell. When the stock market, or a particular stock, is very volatile, your selling price can change significantly throughout the day.

For example, the stock of an individual company may start the trading day at a price of $40 per share, rise to $45 by the middle of the day, and then fall to $37.50 by the end of the day. A simple calculation shows how time can affect the amount of money you may make from selling 100 shares: from an early morning $4,000, to an afternoon $4,500, to a day's end $3,750.

When you want to redeem (that is, sell) shares of a mutual fund, the time of the day when you submit your request (by phone, fax, Internet, or mail) doesn't matter. Although the net asset value (NAV) of the fund (as we explain in Chapter 2) may rise and fall throughout the day, you always end up receiving a cheque based on the closing price for the end of the trading day (4 p.m. Eastern Time).

Warning

Carefully read about the redemption of units in your fund's prospectus. Some funds require that your redemption order be in writing and reserve the right to request formal confirmation of your identity (for example, having your signature guaranteed by a financial institution). The redemption order may not be executed until a day after all the particulars are in place, and your payout may not occur for several more days (in other words, redemption does not mean "instant cash"). In addition, keep your eyes open for any early redemption penalties such as a two percent charge for selling your units before 90 days.

No maturity dates

Another disadvantage of mutual funds relates specifically to bond funds — that is, funds that specialize in bonds rather than stocks or other investments. Typically, when you invest in an individual bond, you are given a *maturity date* — that is, the date when the loan represented by the bond comes due. On that date, you get back the amount you paid for the bond (the *principal*), plus interest. The return is certain, unless the company that issued the bond runs into financial difficulties — Government of Canada bonds are 100 percent safe because of the government's ability to raise money through taxation.

An investment in a bond fund works differently. The fund manager is continually buying and selling bonds with a variety of maturity dates. Periodically, you receive a portion of the interest earned by the fund. However, no specific maturity date exists for your shares in the fund, and thus no certainty about the amount you can expect to receive when you decide to sell your shares. You may end up selling your shares in the fund for more or for less than you paid.

CHAPTER 4
LOOKING AT EQUITY FUNDS

IN THIS CHAPTER

- Sizing up equity funds
- Examining equity funds
- Picking the type of equity fund that's right for you

Mutual funds come in many flavours, and clever folks are inventing new, specialized types of funds all the time. Which kinds of funds are right for you? In this chapter, we explain some of the more popular types of funds and suggest which investors ought to be most interested in which fund types.

Defining Equity Mutual Funds

Equity mutual funds (sometimes also referred to as stock or growth mutual funds) invest primarily in common shares of domestic and foreign corporations (also referred to as equities).

Although you can find many specific types of equity funds with widely varying risk and reward characteristics, equity funds in general outperform bond funds. Equity funds are top performers because they're invested in the stock market, which has proven, over many decades, to be the world's fastest-growing investment arena.

Although returns on equity funds haven't been as impressive as in the United States (where returns are around 15 percent), on a 10-year basis to June 30, 1998, funds invested primarily in Canadian equities had annual average returns of 10.6

percent. By comparison, bond funds averaged 9.3 percent, and money market funds 6.6 percent. (Chapter 5 contains detailed descriptions of both bond and money market funds.)

However, a tradeoff is involved. The higher growth of equity funds comes with somewhat greater risk. Equity funds may rise or fall, depending on the behaviour of the overall stock market, of particular industries, or of the specific companies selected by the fund manager. In a prolonged bear (declining) market, equity funds may even stagnate for a period of months or years.

The longer your investment horizon (that is, the more you are focused on long-term rather than short-term investment goals), the more appropriate equity funds are for your portfolio. If you expect to cash in your investment within the next three years, you should consider keeping all or most of your money out of equity funds. In fact, if you need money for a specific short-term goal, you may just want to stick to either a federal government bond or a corporate bond. These bonds provide fixed interest income and when they are held to maturity, you get 100 percent of your principal back. Not all equity funds behave alike, as shown in Figure 4-1. Wide variations are possible among stock funds in terms of risk, volatility, and growth potential. The following sections highlight

Figure 4-1: Sample annual returns for various fund categories. Past returns do not guarantee future returns.

Annual Returns

	1 year	5 year	10 year
Stock (Equity) Mutual Funds	11.98%	18.01%	15.75%
Index Funds	31.44%	26.47%	21.13%
Small Cap Funds	(9.49%)	17.34%	14.21%
Growth Funds	(25.15%)	20.49%	17.91%
Growth and Income Funds	(18.69%)	20.54%	17.30%
International Mutual Funds	(14.32%)	8.29%	9.48%

some common types of stock funds, with explanations of how each kind of fund can be expected to perform.

Index Funds

To understand index funds, you must first understand what a stock market index is.

A stock market *index* is a list of stocks whose combined performance is tracked by investors as an indication of the health of a particular portion of the economy.

Even people who know little or nothing about the stock market have heard of some of the more famous indexes. In the United States, the best-known index is the Dow Jones Industrial Average (DJIA), which is a selection of 30 corporations trading on the New York Stock Exchange. In Canada, the TSE 300 composite is the best-known index. It consists of the 300 stocks with the largest *market capitalization* (or value of outstanding stock as explained later in this chapter) traded on the Toronto Stock Exchange (TSE), and is divided into 14 major industry groups. As the value of the companies in these groups rises and falls, the TSE 300 rises and falls with them. In addition to the TSE 300, the Toronto Stock Exchange features numerous other indexes including the S&P(Standard and Poor's)/TSE 60, which consists of 60 of the largest and most liquid stocks traded on the exchange. Other Canadian exchanges such as Vancouver (VSE), Alberta (ASE), and Montreal (ME) also boast indexes of their own.

An *index fund* tracks the return on a benchmark index, which represents the average return for a market. The manager of an index fund buys the stocks contained in a particular index. For example, the Great-West Life Equity Index Fund — the granddaddy of Canadian index funds founded in 1983, currently with a total asset size of over $55 million — is based on the TSE 300 composite index. The investment objective of an index fund depends on the index being followed.

A broad index reflects changes in the overall economy, which usually moves more gradually than any single business sector. Thus, a broad index is usually less volatile than a more narrow one; and so, in general, the broader the index, the more conservative the fund. Index funds are available today based on every popular stock market index.

As you may imagine, managing an index fund is less challenging than managing most other fund types. The manager of an index fund is simply charged with buying and selling stocks to match those contained in its index. This style of fund management is sometimes called *passive investing* or *closet indexing*. By contrast, other funds are run by managers who must constantly make independent investment decisions; this style is known as *active investing*.

Because closet indexing calls for less complicated managerial decisions, the cost of running an index fund is less than with other fund types. Thus, investors in index funds generally incur lower management fees (see Chapter 6).

In general, index funds perform well; in fact, the majority of funds that are actively managed actually grow less quickly than such broad indexes as the TSE 300 "Beating the indexes" isn't an easy challenge, even for a highly-skilled professional money manager. So index fund investing has become a particularly popular choice among investors who want to enjoy some of the strong growth possible in the stock market while minimizing the risks that go with active management.

Because closet indexed funds trade less often than actively managed funds, index funds generate less capital gain income than most other funds (check out Chapter 2). This is a tax benefit for most investors, as explained in Chapter 9.

Small Cap Funds

Some stock mutual funds are characterized by the *market capitalization* of the companies whose shares they own. Market capitalization is the value that the stock market assigns to a company, derived by multiplying the stock price by the total number of shares.

For example, if a particular company's stock has a current price of $42 per share, and 10 million shares of stock are held by investors, the company's market capitalization would equal $42 × 10 million = $420 million. Theoretically, this is the purchase price to buy all the shares of the company on the open market.

A *small cap fund* specializes in companies with a relatively small market capitalization — usually below $300 million. Some small cap funds focus on start-up companies, often in new or emerging industries such as high technology. Others focus on established companies that have plenty of room for growth. The smaller firms whose stock is owned by a small cap fund can be very profitable investments, but they can also be risky. If the company managers make a few mistakes — expanding too quickly, for example, or sinking too much money into an unproven technology — the firm may go bankrupt. Thus, the manager of a small cap fund needs to have a shrewd sense of business judgment in order to separate the truly promising small firms from those that are shaky.

Tip

You may want to put a portion of your investment money into a small cap fund — but not all of it. For example, if you invest 20 percent of your savings in a small cap fund, you have the opportunity to enjoy rapid growth if the fund does well, without running the risk of losing your whole retirement or education portfolio if the fund runs into bad luck.

Large Cap Funds

A *large cap fund* specializes in stocks with a market value of $1 billion or more. Such a fund focuses on large, well-established companies, which tend to have lower risk than small companies. Large firms also often provide dividend income, which smaller and newer firms rarely do (see Chapter 2). Examples of large cap companies are BCE Inc. and Power Corporation of Canada. (They are also known as *blue chip* stocks, named after the most expensive chips used for gambling games like poker.)

As always, the benefits of large cap funds come with trade-offs. Although a large cap fund is relatively low-risk, growth is likely to be steady but slow in most economic circumstances. A big, old company like General Motors has a well-established position in the auto marketplace, and the number of cars sold in North America or the world is probably not going to double or triple in the next five years.

By contrast, sales could grow that quickly in a brand-new industry such as biotechnology. Thus, a large cap fund is a good choice for a more conservative investor, or for that portion of your portfolio that you don't want to take chances with. (These generalizations don't always hold true. At times, large cap funds actually grow more quickly than small cap funds. But such times are the exception rather than the rule.)

Mid Cap Funds

As its name suggests, a *mid cap stock fund* (also known as medium cap) falls between small cap and large cap funds, usually owning shares in companies that have market capitalization between $300 million and $500 million, although there are no set standards. Some business sectors that contain mid cap stocks are utility companies (such as oil, gas, and electric companies), service companies (such as retail chains), and some technology companies.

Mid cap fund performance tends to fall between that of small and large companies, too: mid caps face less risk of failure than small cap stocks, but have better earnings potential than large cap stocks.

Growth Funds

A *growth fund* is an equity fund managed primarily in pursuit of capital gains — that is, most of the profit sought by the manager takes the form of higher share prices rather than dividends paid. The manager of a growth fund is interested in finding industries that are rapidly expanding due to economic, business, or social trends and individual companies that are managed so effectively that they are growing quickly.

A growth fund may invest in stocks of large, small, or mid cap companies. The success of the fund depends heavily on the expertise of its manager and his ability to pick winners from among the many companies competing in a particular industry.

For example, one industry for which many economists predict a bright future over the next two decades is pharmaceuticals, which manufacture drugs, medicines, and other health-related products. As the large baby boom generation born in the 1940s and 1950s ages, their need for medical care is likely to increase, and pharmaceutical companies are positioned to enjoy growing sales and profits.

The manager of a growth fund probably wants to follow the pharmaceutical industry closely. However, to be successful, the fund manager also needs to identify the individual companies in the industry whose stock is likely to perform best.

Key to successful fund management is staying informed about the management of the leading pharmaceutical firms and listening for news about breakthrough medicines in development at each company.

The growth fund manager who can accurately guess which firms are destined to do well in the years to come will make profitable stock selections, and investors in his fund will benefit accordingly.

A growth fund is usually a good investment for the long-term investor. For example, if you're investing for a retirement that is 20 years or more in the future, you may want to put half or more of your investment money into a growth fund, which should benefit from upward trends in the economy during the coming decades.

Aggressive Growth Funds

If a growth fund seeks companies that can grow at 80 kilometres per hour, an *aggressive growth fund* is like a race-car driver. The manager of such a fund buys stocks she thinks have the most exciting growth possibilities, including small cap stocks, stocks of companies that are developing new technologies, and stocks in firms whose business is likely to double or triple within a few years.

In pursuit of higher returns, aggressive growth funds take greater risks and are subject to greater volatility. If you invest in an aggressive growth fund, your money may shrink by 50 percent one year and grow by 100 percent the next. Don't pick this kind of fund unless you can handle a financial roller-coaster ride.

An aggressive growth fund also may use financial techniques that involve more risk. One example is the use of *options* and other so-called *derivative instruments*. When an investor buys an option, he buys the right to buy or sell a stock (or other security) at a prespecified price at some time in the future.

In effect, an option is a bet that the price of a security will move in a specific direction, up or down. If the investor bets right, the profits can be large; if he bets wrong, the losses can be just as large.

Warning

If you suspect that a mutual fund is being managed in a high-risk fashion, study the prospectus carefully. If the document indicates that the fund manager is investing in options, futures, or other derivative instruments, make sure you understand the degree and nature of the financial risk involved. And don't invest more money than you can afford to lose. Gambling a little can be fun — but not with the money you're relying on for retirement or your kids' education.

Growth and Income Funds

A *growth and income fund* is generally lower in risk than a growth fund. Such a fund invests in companies that have good growth potential but also pay dividends to their investors (more on the subject in Chapter 2).

The fact that the fund profits in at least two ways from its investments cushions volatility, making it more of an "all-weather" fund than the more uncertain growth fund. This type of fund is less volatile because the dividends keep coming even if the stock price goes down.

In most cases, stock dividends represent a relatively minor portion of the profits you make from a mutual fund. In 1998, for example, stocks listed in the TSE 300 composite index paid an average dividend of about 1.5 percent. (Thus, if you owned a share of stock priced at $75 that paid the average dividend, you'd receive, in the course of the year, cheques totaling $1.13 per share — not a huge sum by any standard.) On the other hand, the average dividend yield from an aggressive growth fund in the same year was just 0.3 percent.

Obviously, if the security of knowing that dividends are rolling in is important to you, stay with a growth and income fund rather than seeking aggressive growth.

International Mutual Funds

More and more investors today are seeking investment opportunities outside Canada. This makes economic sense. Although Canada is still a dynamic, growing nation, it's also a mature country, whose business, social, and economic structures are largely in place.

By contrast, some other regions of the world have the potential of growing much more quickly in the years ahead, as they try to rapidly catch up to more developed nations in terms of industry and consumer spending.

Investors seeking growth opportunities should consider putting at least part of their money into *international* or *global mutual funds,* which specialize in foreign investments.

Naturally, international investing involves many complexities. Someone who invests in foreign stocks has to worry about foreign economies, interest rates, tax laws, political conditions, and business practices. But with an international mutual fund, the fund manager does all the research — and the worrying — for you. You gain exposure to overseas opportunities without the headaches.

One type of risk that is unique to international investing is *currency risk.* When you put $1,000 in an international fund, you are, in effect, buying foreign currency, because the fund has to change your dollars into German marks, Russian rubles, Indian rupees, or some other foreign money before it can be invested.

As you know, the *exchange rate* between Canadian currency and other currencies is constantly in flux, based mainly on changes in the world and local economies. One day, the Canadian dollar may be worth 70 Japanese yen; the next day, it may rise to 85 yen. When the Canadian dollar is up, the relative value of your foreign holdings will go down. On the other hand, when the dollar drops, your foreign currencies go up, which is an added benefit to your portfolio.

To minimize the dangers of currency risk, try to limit your international investing to long-term money — funds you won't need to withdraw quickly. By exercising patience, you can wait for a favourable movement in currency values before you sell your shares. Also, try to diversify your international holdings. Pick funds that invest in several international economies rather than just one. Currency losses in one country can offset profits in another.

International funds include funds that invest in specific countries, such as England or Japan, as well as regional funds. The term *global* is generally used to describe funds that invest in Canadian companies as well as foreign ones.

Canada's Income Tax Act has very sticky regulations about foreign investments both inside and outside RRSPs. See Chapter 9 for a full explanation of what you can and can't do with international holdings.

Emerging Market Mutual Funds

An *emerging market mutual fund* is a type of international fund that invests in so-called emerging markets, such as Latin America, Africa, Southeast Asia, the Middle East, and Eastern Europe.

Emerging market funds are relatively risky for several reasons. Currency values are often volatile, making currency risk greater than with the developed nations of Europe or Asia; political problems are more likely, which can affect the economic prospects of a country and therefore the value of your investments. In addition, stock markets in emerging nations are usually less liquid because you have fewer investors looking for stocks to buy.

You can make big returns from an emerging market fund, especially if your fund's manager is fortunate enough to pick countries or companies that are on the verge of successful business breakthroughs.

But the potential for large losses is always present. Consider investing part of your portfolio in an emerging market fund, but only a portion that you can afford to lose. Again, consult Chapter 9 to find out about tax implications on investing outside of Canada.

Specialty Funds

A *specialty fund* or *sector fund* specializes in stocks from a particular industry. The manager of a specialty fund is an expert on the companies in that industry, its long-term growth prospects, and the business and social trends that are likely to affect it. Consider investing in a specialty fund if you feel a particular business has special potential for success.

Specialty funds can be roughly divided into several categories — precious metals funds, energy funds, natural resource funds, technology funds, small company funds, real estate funds, and health funds.

Because specialty funds concentrate in specific market areas, they are often much more volatile than equity funds, which invest in many industries. Table 4-1 shows the high and low returns for some Canadian specialty funds over a three-year period between 1994 and 1997. Note the extreme volatility of many of the funds during this short period.

Table 4-1:   Highs and Lows of Selected Specialty Funds During a Three-Year Period (1994–1997)

Fund Name	High	Low
AIM Global Health Sciences	84.5%	-2.5%
Altamira S-T Global Income	6.4%	-1.8%
Fonds De Solidarite (Ftq)	14.8%	5.0%
Green Line Science & Tech	62.6%	-9.6%
GT Global Glo Infrastructe	28.5%	0.8%
GT Global Global Telecomm	59.7%	-17.1%
Investors Real Property	6.7%	3.8%
Spectrum Utd. Glo Telecomm	28.9%	-8.6%
Median for Group	28.7%	-2.2%

Remember

Choose a sector fund only if you're prepared to live with similar ups and downs.

CHAPTER 5

FINDING OUT ABOUT FIXED INCOME FUNDS AND BALANCED FUNDS

IN THIS CHAPTER

- Defining three different types of fixed income funds — bond, mortgage, and dividend

- Investing in both stocks and bonds with balanced funds

Fixed income funds and balanced funds are two categories of specialized funds that may fit your investment personality. In this chapter, we explain fixed income funds and balanced funds and suggest when each type of fund is right for you.

Exploring Fixed Income Funds

Fixed income funds aim to provide you with a steady income flow without putting your capital at risk. They do this by assembling a portfolio of income-producing securities that are, for the most part, interest- or dividend-producing investments. There are three basic types of fixed income funds — bond funds, mortgage-based funds, and dividend funds.

Money market funds

A *money market mutual fund* invests in short-term bonds issued by the Canadian government, large corporations, banks, and other rock-solid institutions.

As we explain in Chapter 1, a money market fund is considered a conservative investment with little possibility of losing money; in fact, many investors and financial experts refer to money market funds as a *cash equivalent,* almost as safe and liquid as money in the bank.

Because money market investments are short-term (that is, bonds that are to be paid off within a few weeks or months), they closely reflect current interest rates. Most money market mutual funds are currently earning between 3 percent and 4 percent interest (computed as an annual growth rate).

During the early 1980s, when inflation and interest rates were both very high, money market funds earned over 10 percent annually. Such growth is unlikely to return unless economic conditions change dramatically.

You can invest in money market funds through a mutual fund company or a bank. In most cases, banks pay slightly lower interest rates than mutual fund companies. Also remember that your money market investment through a bank is not insured by the Canada Deposit Insurance Corporation (CDIC), unlike ordinary bank deposits.

A money market fund is a good place to keep money that you may need in a hurry. It's also a handy parking place for money that you plan to invest somewhere, but you just haven't decided exactly where.

For example, Joanne gets a larger-than-expected end-of-year bonus from the company where she works — $2,500. She can deposit the bonus cheque in a money market fund managed by a mutual fund company. It will immediately begin earning about 4 percent interest. Over the next month or two, Joanne can take her time to research other investment opportunities. If she then decides to invest the bonus in a growth fund, for example, she can move the money from the money market fund into the growth fund simply by placing a call to the mutual fund company.

Government bond funds

A *government bond* is an IOU issued by various levels of government, often designed to raise money for a particular purpose. A *government bond fund* invests in a portfolio of such bonds. Bonds issued by the federal and provincial governments are of high credit quality since default is unlikely. Municipal government bonds are usually of lesser quality because the municipal government has limited power when it comes to taxing to repay the debt. You can also get a global government bond fund that invests in high-quality, low-default risk government bonds of major countries — these usually offer high-interest income with potential for both capital and currency gains. The primary objective of any bond fund is income paid from the interest on the loan.

Corporate bond funds

A *corporate bond fund* invests in debt issued by companies that need to raise money. Corporate bonds generally offer a higher yield than government bonds, but have greater default risks. These bonds are rated for safety by the Canadian Bond Rating Service and/or the Dominion Bond Rating Service. One type of corporate bond for most investors to avoid is the so-called *high-yield bond,* also known as a *junk bond.* As the latter name implies, such bonds are very risky. They're offered by companies that are small, sometimes struggling, and prone to great shifts of fortune, either up or down.

Fortunes have been made by high-yield bond investors — and also lost. If you're offered the opportunity to invest in a high-yield bond fund — some high-yield bonds do well in bond funds — examine it cautiously, and only invest money that you can afford to lose. It may happen.

Because investors are wary of high-yield or junk bonds, some brokers or other bond funds salespeople may try to sell you a high-yield bond fund without identifying it as such. If you are offered shares in a bond fund with an interest rate two or three percentage points higher than other funds you are considering, be careful! Chances are that the risk associated with the fund is very high, even if the salesperson doesn't reveal the fact.

Mortgage funds

A *mortgage* is a loan secured by property. A *mortgage fund* invests primarily in top-quality, single-family Canadian residential first mortgages — guaranteed against default by the issuing bank or Canada Mortgage and Housing Corporation (CMHC) — from mortgage lenders, and thereby acquires the right to receive payments from borrowers. Mortgage funds are designed to provide maximum interest income for investors, as typically the yield on mortgages is higher than the yield on bonds to compensate for additional risks.

A *mortgage-backed security fund* (MBS) is securities backed by a pool of residential mortgages guaranteed by Canada Mortgage and Housing Corporation. MBSs generally offer the highest yields among the highest-rated fixed income securities, but tend to carry somewhat higher management costs.

Because mortgage interest rates are almost always higher than bonds, mortgage funds are worth a look if you require income for your current needs or if you are seeking a conservative investment for retirement savings.

Dividend funds

A *dividend fund* invests mainly in high-quality preferred shares and high-yielding common shares (a preferred share is stock in a company that entitles the owner to certain specified rights such as the right to recieve dividends, while a common share represents a basic unit of ownership in the company with no special privileges). A dividend fund's primary objective is to generate a high level of after tax income. To encourage Canadians to invest in shares and to help companies raise capital, the government introduced the federal dividend tax credit to reduce the tax rate on dividend income from Canadian corporations. You can use dividend funds to earn higher after-tax returns than are available from bond and mortgage funds — perfect if you're looking for a healthy income stream. See Chapter 9 for further details.

Learning about Balanced Funds

A *balanced fund* owns both stocks and bonds. It's a conservative type of fund investment, one that attempts to make it easy for investors to enjoy some of the safety of bonds along with the growth potential of stocks through a single investment.

The typical balanced fund is 60 percent invested in stocks and 40 percent in bonds. Its investment objective is to preserve principal (that is, avoid losing any of the money invested), pay current income (that is, dividends), and achieve long-term growth.

If you're a brand-new investor, a balanced fund can be an easy, safe choice. If you have a little more experience, consider creating your own "balanced" fund by dividing your money between stock and bond funds of your choice.

By selecting funds that closely fit your own investment goals, you're likely to achieve better results than you can get from a prepackaged balanced fund.

Figure 5-1 shows a comparison of average annual total returns of bond and balanced fund categories, covering both short-term (1 year) and longer-term (5 and 10 year) performance. (Be sure to base your investment research on current performance information.)

Figure 5-1: Sample annual returns for various funds, including balanced funds. Past returns do not guarantee future returns.

Annual Returns

	1 year	5 year	10 year
Fixed Income (Bond) Funds	9.56%	8.00%	10.19%
Money Market Funds	5.57%	5.62%	5.98%
Government Bond Funds	6.63%	5.67%	8.23%
Corporate Bond Funds	8.22%	6.95%	9.38%
Balanced Funds	14.83%	14.73%	14.09%

CHAPTER 6

UNCOVERING MUTUAL FUND FEES AND EXPENSES

IN THIS CHAPTER

- Comparing load and no-load funds
- Evaluating your investment expenses
- Looking out for trailer fees
- Tuning in to turnover

Although mutual funds provide many benefits to the individual investor, these benefits aren't free for the asking. Buying and owning a mutual fund involves costs, which can greatly affect the profitability of a given investment. Fortunately, these expenses are evident if you study the fund's prospectus, so you never have to make an uninformed decision about what costs you're willing to carry.

Load versus No-Load Funds

Soon after you begin reading about the world of mutual funds, you're sure to encounter the distinction between *load* and *no-load funds*. The difference between them is important.

Load funds

A *load* is a sales charge or commission payable to the person who sells you a mutual fund. A *load fund* is a mutual fund on which such fees are charged.

Typically, a financial professional sells a load fund. Some load funds are sold by *full-service brokers* — salespeople who advise you on your investment choices, provide you with brochures and research reports, and pocket a commission in return for their work. Financial planners, bankers, insurance agents, and other financial professionals also sell load funds.

All load funds carry attached sales commissions, usually representing anywhere from 2 percent to 9 percent of your investment. For example, if you invest $1,000 in a certain load stock fund with a 5.75 percent sales charge, $57.50 comes off the top to pay the broker. The remaining $942.50 is your investment in the mutual fund itself. When a sales commission is paid upon initial investment in the fund, it is called a *front-end load.*

Back-end load

Instead of upfront sales charges, some load funds charge a *back-end load,* also known as a *rear load, deferred sales charge,* or *redemption fee.* With this kind of load, you pay a fee when you cash out of the fund by selling your shares. The size of the redemption fee depends on the fund you are invested in; each fund has its own fee structure, often on a sliding scale, so that the redemption fee decreases the longer you hold the fund.

For example, a typical back-end load structure provides that, if you redeem your mutual fund shares within a six-year window, you can expect to pay anywhere from 6 percent to 1 percent — 6 percent during the first year, 5 percent during the second year, and so on. The back-end load drops off at the seventh year. (By design, the fee structure encourages you to hold on to your investment for a longer time, which benefits the fund company and you.)

Carefully study the sales brochure or prospectus (see Chapter 7) for any fund you're thinking of investing in. Make sure you understand the nature, size, and structure of any load charge.

Some load funds impose front-end (upfront) sales charges; others include back-end loads or deferred charges; and still others impose various combinations of these charges. Read the fine print so you won't be blindsided by unanticipated expenses.

No-load funds

A *no-load fund* charges no sales commission. Typically, the mutual fund firm that sponsors the fund is the investor's source for this kind of fund. These firms often sponsor entire families of no-load funds, each with a different investment objective, philosophy, and style.

Although no-load funds are still outnumbered by load funds in Canada, they are on the rise as more banks and trust companies get into the mutual fund business. Mutual fund families such as Altamira, Sceptre, and Phillips, Hager & North offer a wide array of no-load funds, one of which is likely to be an appropriate and attractive investment for you.

When you invest in a no-load fund, you skip the middleman — the sales agent — and therefore save the money that would otherwise go to pay his commission. You don't have to meet with or speak to a broker or salesperson; instead, you call the mutual fund company, ask for an application and informational brochures about their funds, and then send in a completed application form with your cheque. If you invest $1,000, the entire amount begins working for you, with no deduction for any load or commission.

Is there any significant downside to choosing a no-load fund? Not really. Some investors prefer load funds because they like having an ongoing relationship with a broker or other financial professional who can advise them from time to time.

By contrast, with a no-load fund, the investor is on her own; she can call the fund company to make transactions or to request publications, but she can count on speaking to a different representative every time she calls.

Some no-load fund companies that do not pay any *trailer fees,* which we explain later in this chapter, or commissions to salespeople for pushing its fund, will allow brokers and other financial advisors to add up to 2 percent as a front-end fee, especially when they give advice. This fact is not advertised to the general public.

The investment performance of load and no-load funds is the subject of many research studies. In virtually every study, no significant difference is apparent. In other words, investors who paid sales commissions of 5 percent or more for load funds did *not* enjoy noticeably better investment results.

Because you can invest your money with equal profit in either a load or a no-load fund, why not save some of your hard-earned cash by considering only no-load funds for your portfolio? (But before deciding, consider the impact of trailer fees. These particular fees may tip the scales against certain no-load funds.)

If you do choose a load fund, keep in mind that the load is the maximum — not the required — sales commission allowed. If you have enough business to offer them, some advisors and brokers may lower the load or waive it altogether, because they receive trailer fees as long as you keep your money in the fund.

Annual Operating Expenses

Of course, (almost) no good thing is free. All mutual funds have associated expenses — even no-load funds (see Figure 6-1). Before choosing any fund, learn about the costs you can expect to pay for the investment expertise and services the fund provides.

Figure 6-1: Typical fees and expenses of a fund.

Fees and Expenses

Unitholder Fees *(fees paid directly from your investment)*

Sales Charge (Front-End Load):		5.0%
Redemption Charge	5.5%	(if sold within 1 year after purchase)
(Back-End Load):	5.5%	(if sold within 2 years after purchase)
	4.5%	(if sold within 3 years after purchase)
	4.0%	(if sold within 4 years after purchase)
	3.5%	(if sold within 5 years after purchase)
	2.5%	(if sold within 6 years after purchase)
	1.5%	(if sold within 4 years after purchase)
	Nil	(if sold after 7 years)
Exchange Fees:		2.0%

Annual Fund Operating Expenses
(expenses deducted from the fund's assets)

Annual Management Fee:	2.0%
Administrative Expenses:	0.2%
Total Annual Fund Operating Expenses:	2.2%

*Some funds offer choice of either a front-end or back-end load charge

You can find the *annual operating expenses* of any fund described and estimated as an annual percentage of your investment in the fund's prospectus (see Chapter 7). These expenses may include management fees, administrative costs, trailer fees, all of which we explain in this chapter. These fees are generally deducted automatically from your account and shown when you receive your regular account statement in the mail, so you don't have to worry about sending in a cheque. And because the expenses are charged on a daily basis, you also don't have to worry about trying to get out of a fund before these fees are deducted.

Some funds are naturally more expensive to operate than others. A fund that invests in international stocks or small company stocks tends to be more expensive than average because research costs are likely to be higher in these areas.

By contrast, an index fund that simply tracks the performance of a preselected bundle of stocks generally has lower expenses and therefore can save you money when you invest. While a fund with higher expenses may more than make up for them with a higher investment return, this is not always the case. In fact, funds with higher operating expenses often produce lower rates of return because the expenses are deducted from the returns that a fund generates.

Stick with funds that maintain low annual operating expenses. Like loads or sales charges, these fees come out of your pocket and reduce your rate of return.

Management fees

Management fees cover the fund company's management expenses — the work of lawyers and accountants, the cost of maintaining books and records, money spent complying with government regulations and disclosure rules, research expenses, and the salary of the fund manager, among other costs. The amount varies from fund to fund and from one type of fund to another.

Management fees are usually lower on money market mutual funds and other bond funds, and higher on most types of equity funds because of the greater complexity of the investment decisions.

Management fees are usually the single largest portion of a fund's annual expenses, averaging between 0.5 percent and up to 3.0 percent of the fund's assets.

Administrative costs

Administrative costs may include a variety of expenses that are basically user fees. Some funds — especially no-load funds — levy a one-time charge for opening an account with a company. This charge is called a *set-up fee* and is usually between $25 and $50. Once your account is set up, you may be allowed to switch from one fund to another within the same company, but may also be charged a *switching fee*. Some funds allow a certain number of free switches each year and thereafter may apply a $10 or $15 fee for each subsequent switch.

For investors who wish to receive regular payments from their fund, a *systematic withdrawal charge* may be applied either annually, on a per withdrawal basis, or by using some or combination of the two. If a fund is held as a RRSP or RRIF, many funds impose an *administrative* or *trustee fee* ranging from $15 to $75 per year.

Remember

Depending on the funds you hold, you may face various additional administrative costs. Because the fees vary from fund to fund, it is important to understand before buying what you will be responsible for, information that is fully disclosed in the fund's prospectus. (For tips on reading a fund's prospectus, see Chapter 7.)

The management expense ratio

One handy way to measure the relative cost of investing in a particular fund is by looking at its *management expense ratio* (MER). This figure, which appears in the fee table section of the fund's prospectus (see Chapter 7), is the amount that each investor can expect to pay for fund expenses each year, stated as a percentage of the money invested.

The MER includes almost all fees — both management and administrative — but does not include sales charges or specific fees such as an RRSP trustee fee. Because some funds pay expenses out of their management fee and some charge expenses directly to the fund, the MER is relatively all-inclusive and allows useful comparison amongst other funds.

MERs for equity funds range from 0.75 percent to over 3.0 percent, while MERs for income funds are marginally lower. Table 6-1 shows MERs for some common types of funds.

Table 6-1:   Mutual Fund Management Expense Ratios (MERs) for Selected Fund Types

Fund Type	Management Expense Ratio Range (Given as a Percentage of Invested Funds)
Canadian Bonds (fixed income)	0.68% to 2.21%
Canadian Equities	1.13% to 2.59%
Canadian Balanced	1.31% to 2.45%
US Equity	1.19% to 2.62%
Global Equity	1.22% to 2.43%
Asian Equity	2.39% to 3.11%

Source: John Nicola Financial Group Ltd.

Low-loads and trailer fees

A low-load fund is a relatively new type of fund which typically charges a very low (around 1.0 percent) front-end charge. The broker or dealer then receives additional compensation in the form of *trailer fees,* which are paid by the manager of the fund out of the management fee. Trailer fees (or service fees) are commissions paid to the dealer on a continuing basis and run anywhere from 0.25 percent to 1.0 percent of assets. Even some no-load funds pay trailer fees.

Naturally, the lower the trailer fees charged by the fund, the better. In general, no-load and low-load funds are a better bargain than load funds. However, you may find that, in some instances, a load fund may actually be a better buy than a fund with a heavy trailer.

Suppose you're considering a fund with a modest front-end load (say, less than 5 percent). Because the front-end load is a one-time payment, while trailer fees are an ongoing annual charge paid out of the management fee, which therefore cuts into your return, the front-end load may end up costing you less, especially if you plan to keep your investment for a long time.

In effect, the existence of trailer fees gives the investor a choice of whether to pay sales expenses up-front, or have them debited as an expense later on a regular basis. Look closely at trailer fees before making an investment decision — they may influence you to choose one fund over another.

The cost of turnover

Another cost of investing that doesn't show up in the expense ratio of a fund is the cost of *turnover*. Turnover is the rate at which a fund buys and sells investments. A turnover rate of 100 percent means that, on average, the fund manager buys and sells stocks or bonds with a value equivalent to that of the entire investment portfolio each year.

Every time the fund manager buys or sells a stock or bond, she incurs expenses — brokerage commissions and other administrative costs. The higher the turnover rate, the more frequent trading of securities the manager is engaged in, and the higher the trading costs. Over time, high turnover can be a significant drag on the profits of a fund.

You can find the fund's turnover rate in its prospectus (see Chapter 7). The least actively managed funds, such as an index fund, may have a very low turnover rate of just 5 percent to 10 percent. A very actively managed fund may have a turnover rate of 500 percent or more, meaning that each security in the fund is held, on average, for just about one-fifth of a year — 10 weeks or so — before being sold.

In general, turnover rates of less than 30 percent are considered low; 30 percent to 100 percent is average; over 100 percent is high. A typical Canadian equity fund has a turnover rate of approximately 35 percent.

If every other comparative point is equal, choose a fund with a lower turnover rate because more efficient fund management is likely to earn you greater profits in the long run.

CHAPTER 7

RESEARCHING A MUTUAL FUND

IN THIS CHAPTER

- Matching investment goals with fund categories
- Finding high-performance funds
- Evaluating fund management
- Reading the fund prospectus

With the multitude of mutual funds available today, you can easily feel overwhelmed when it comes to choosing one, two, or a few for your investment dollars. You can get off to a good start by knowing what you are trying to achieve by investing.

As we suggest in Chapter 1, the new investor can begin by listing his or her financial goals and deciding whether they are mainly long-term goals, short-terms goals, or a mixture of both. When you know your investment objectives, you can focus on specific types of funds, narrowing the universe from which you have to choose.

Matching Investment Goals with Fund Categories

The following checklist contains some specific suggestions that can help you decide which types of funds may best suit your personal situation and investment goals:

- If your investment goals are mainly *long-term,* consider *equity funds.*

- If your investment goals are mainly short-term, fixed income funds such as government bond funds or money-market funds.

- If you feel able to tolerate a relatively high degree of risk, consider growth funds, aggressive growth funds, emerging market funds, or mid cap and small cap funds.

- If minimizing risk is important to you, consider bond funds (including corporate bond funds), balanced funds, growth and income funds, or large cap funds.

- If you want to target specific regions or industries you think will grow, consider international or sector funds.

- If you want to minimize the costs of investing, consider index funds.

- If you want to minimize the taxes on your investment profits, consider dividend funds.

You can find more details on each of these fund types in Chapters 4 and 5.

Obviously, overlap exists among these various personal goals. A single investor — call him Matthew for the sake of illustration — may have two or three different yet complementary investment preferences.

For example, say he wants to invest for the long-term goal of retirement, to minimize risk, and to minimize the tax bite on his investment profits. In light of these three preferences, Matthew may want to consider more than one category of funds, looking for the fund type that offers a comfortable balance among different factors. So zeroing in on one category of fund isn't necessarily an obvious or easy process. The checklist above can help you begin the process of sorting out the possibilities.

Finding High-Performing Funds

After you decide which categories of funds are likely to be best for you, you can begin to narrow your choices still further.

One way to start is by looking at the track record of a wide selection of funds in a particular category. Sources abound for this information.

Magazines that deal with personal finance and investing topics, such as *IE: Money, Canadian Moneysaver,* and *Mutual Fund Review,* run periodic special reports showing comparative investment results for hundreds of mutual funds. The publications usually group the funds by category, so you can quickly zero in on growth funds, index funds, municipal bond funds, or any other fund type of interest to you.

Similar reports appear periodically in business magazines like *Report on Business* and *Canadian Business.* The business sections of both the *National Post* and *The Globe and Mail* also feature daily data galore and periodic full-section mutual fund reports. Visit your local library and ask a librarian to help you locate the most recent mutual fund issues of your favourite financial periodical or check out the publication online. The data you need ought to be easy to find. (The Resource Centre at the back of this book lists many sources of mutual fund information you're sure to find helpful.)

Be sure to compare the one-year, three-year, five-year, and ten-year annualized returns for funds in the specific type or types of funds you are considering (see Figure 7-1). Look for consistently strong results. The fund that amassed huge profits over the past 12 months may have done poorly in previous years, suggesting that next year's performance may lag again.

Figure 7-1: A Sample Performance Report.

Performance/Risk Information

The bar chart below provides an indication of the risk of investing in the fund. The bar chart shows the fund's performance over the last 10 years. Remember that the fund's past performance does not indicate how it will perform in the future.

Annual Total Returns

Year	Return
1989	3.27%
1990	1.21%
1991	-.29%
1992	8.70%
1993	5.47%
1994	6.12%
1995	6.39%
1996	5.58%
1997	6.06%
1998	7.11%

A better bet is a fund that shows an above-average performance year in, year out, for the past five years or more. In this chapter, we give you more suggestions about how to evaluate the track record of a particular mutual fund.

Evaluating Fund Management

By studying the track records of funds in the categories you're interested in, you can identify a handful of strong candidates to focus on even more closely. The next step is to examine the management of those funds, looking for signs of strength and weakness that may guide an investment decision.

Several Canadian firms, such as Portfolio Analytics and BellCharts, specialize in monitoring and tracking mutual funds and publishing reports. Both companies can be accessed online, where a wealth of fund information awaits at sites such as Globefund (www.globefund.com) and The

Fund Library (www.fundlibrary.com). If you prefer the old-fashioned way, Southam publishes its *Sourcebook*, which is available at most libraries and bookstores, and The Fund Counsel (www.fundcounsel.com) sends out a newsletter loaded with information and advice.

Below are some of the questions to ask about any fund that you are seriously considering buying. Information services like those provided by Portfolio Analytics, Southam, and so on either online or in print can provide the answers.

Who is the fund manager? How long has this individual managed the fund? How does the growth record of the fund under this person's management compare to that of other funds?

In general, you want the manager to have a record of at least five years with the fund company, preferably ten or more. If the manager has only been with the firm for two years, his track record is too short to be truly meaningful; any success the fund is currently enjoying may be due more to the efforts of his predecessor. Information about fund managers often is readily available in the financial press — see the Resource Centre at the back of this book for a list of financial magazines and newspapers. Also check online or in any index of newspapers and magazines (available at your local library) for articles about or interviews with the managers of the funds you are considering. You may be able to locate one or more profiles in which the fund manager offers his investment philosophy, explains his successes and failures, and indicates some of his strategies for the months and years to come.

Do the investments currently held by the fund match the fund's stated objectives?

Fund management may not exactly match an advertised description. Some funds touted in advertising as low-risk or conservative investments may actually include some riskier derivatives and other less-than-secure holdings in their portfolios.

Other funds whose names imply "equity" or "stock" may maintain a large portion of their holdings in cash-equivalent investments such as short-term bonds, although in fairness, many fund managers will hold 5 percent to 10 percent in cash for fetching bargains whenever they appear. That said, you still can't assume that the name of a fund offers a fair description of its investment approach.

In order to determine whether the fund manager is investing according to the fund's stated investment objective, you may want to look at a breakdown of the fund's holdings.

Some mutual fund tracking firms offer these breakdowns; you can find similar data in the fund's prospectus (see "Reading the Fund Prospectus" later in this chapter). By looking at the current holdings of the fund, you can gauge how much is held in stocks or bonds and what portions of the fund are invested in various categories of companies — small cap versus large cap stocks, foreign stocks, high-tech businesses, blue chip companies, and so on (as we explain in Chapter 4). If you sense a discrepancy between the stated objective of the fund and the kind of securities that the fund actually holds, you may want to question the clarity and consistency of the fund's management.

The online service offered by Portfolio Analytics (see Figure 7-2) features an abundance of information on many different mutual funds and their managers, including the performance history of the fund and its top 10 holdings (top 10 holdings is a good category to look at especially if you're using just one fund family — there is no point in having five funds with all the same top 10 holdings as that just defeats the whole purpose of diversification). The report also details, in multicoloured pie charts, the geographic and asset weights

Figure 7-2: A sample profile from Portfolio Analytics "`www.pal.com`" online information service.

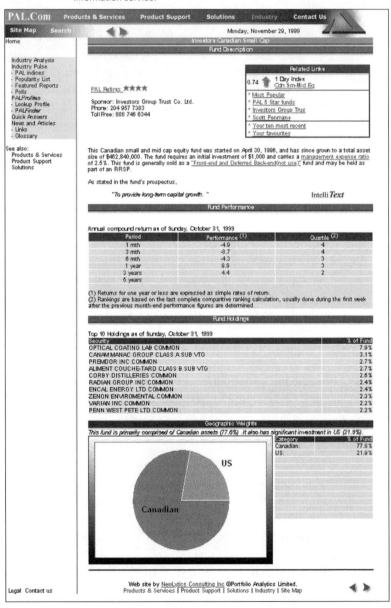

Courtesy of Portfolio Analytics Ltd.

of the fund. All this information should further enlighten you on the objectives of the fund and the style of its manager. You want to feel comfortable with the direction the fund manager generally takes before sending your money to the financial professional for investment.

How do the fund's fees and expenses compare to others in the fund category?

As we explain in Chapter 6, the sales charges, annual expenses, trailer fees, and other costs associated with mutual funds vary widely from fund to fund. Look carefully at these charges and compare them from one fund to another. Be sure that you're aware of the expenses you're going to be responsible for, and factor them into your expectations of investment profit.

You may want to eliminate from consideration any fund with unusually high fees or expenses — unless its investment performance demonstrates consistently better results than other funds in the same category.

Reading the Fund Prospectus

The fund prospectus is a legal document that must contain specific information about a mutual fund. The prospectus informs potential investors about the fund's goals, fees, and expenses, and its investment objectives and degree of risk, as well as information on how to buy and sell shares.

You can obtain a prospectus directly from the fund company or from a broker, financial planner, or other financial professional. Each fund actually has two prospectuses, one being a *simplified prospectus* that attempts to summarize all the main points of the standard prospectus in plain language. After you narrow your fund choices to a handful of possibilities (three to five funds), request prospectuses for each fund and devote an evening to comparing them.

A prospectus is usually not fun to read, but if you know what to look for, you're likely to find that the prospectus contains a wealth of information that can help you decide whether the fund is right for you.

Information contained in the standard prospectus includes

■ The investment objective and practices of the fund

■ An explanation of who is responsible for what, and how administrative and managerial functions are performed

■ The fund's performance history

■ The timing of distributions of the fund's net income

■ The minimum amount of money required to invest

■ The purchaser's statutory rights, including the right to withdraw from an agreement within 48 hours of the purchase

■ The sales charges (loads) associated with investing, and when they are payable — at the front end (upon purchasing shares), at the back end (when selling), or both

■ The fund's operating expenses, including management fees, administrative expenses, and trailer fees

■ How to buy and sell shares and a description of shareholder services provided

■ The risks involved in investing in the fund (there are few specific requirements for this disclosure, so buyer beware)

Remember

The prospectus is not the only source of information you should consult before making a buying decision. Additional information is available in the annual information form, which can be obtained by writing to the issuer of the fund. When you actually buy a fund, the seller is required by law to provide a prospectus, the latest financial statements, and previous quarterly statements, if any.

The more prospectuses you read, the more familiar you can become with the terminology they use. By comparing prospectuses from several funds, you develop a sense of each fund's different personality. You probably find that one fund feels more comfortable to you than the others, which may be a sign that you've found a good prospect for your first investment experience.

CHAPTER 8

BUYING A MUTUAL FUND

- Determining where, when, and how to buy mutual fund shares

- Buying through a broker

- Explaining share classes and fund supermarkets

- Understanding the advantages of dollar cost averaging

With your research and decision-making accomplished, you are ready to buy! But there are choices to make concerning when and where to make your fund investments. Each mutual fund source has advantages and disadvantages that you'll want to weigh in making these choices. You should also consider using the investment technique, known as *dollar cost averaging,* which is a special fund buying method that can actually increase the rate of profit on your money.

Knowing Where to Buy

Investors use a wide range of channels to purchase mutual funds, but buying the fund through brokers and dealers is the most popular, as you can see from the statistics in Table 8-1. Agencies are companies with their own sales forces who sell their own products exclusively or primarily.

Table 8-1: Where Mutual Funds Are Bought by Percentage of Total Sales

Sales Outlet	Percentage of Total Sales
Brokers/Dealers	47.9%
Banks	26.1%
Agencies	10.1%
Trust Companies	4.7%
Direct to Public	4.2%
Life Insurance Companies	3.2%
Unions/Associations	2.6%
Credit Unions	0.6%

Tip

Buying directly from a fund company has traditionally been the cheapest and most convenient way to buy mutual funds for most investors. But with more banks offering no-load funds, they are becoming just as cheap and convenient. Either way, setting up an account usually involves simply completing an application form and sending in your initial investment in the form of a cheque or transferring it from your account at your bank. Voila! You're an investor — it's that simple.

If you participate in some form of employer-sponsored investment program, as we describe in Chapter 1, you may have the opportunity to buy shares from a fund company indirectly, through your company's investment plan. The paperwork and procedures are quite similar.

Only a couple of the questions on the typical mutual fund application are likely to cause you any confusion. Expect to state how you want any capital gains and dividends handled (see Chapter 2 for more on the subject). You can have these profits paid to you in cash, or automatically reinvested in your account, buying more mutual fund shares.

We recommend that you reinvest profits from capital gains and dividends so that your investment portfolio can benefit from the power of compounding, as we explain in Chapter 1.

The mutual fund application may also ask whether you want to participate in an automatic monthly investment plan. This kind of plan automatically transfers a specified amount of money each month from your chequing account into the mutual fund of your choice.

If you're starting out with an investment program, we strongly recommend that you choose this option. After a few months, you won't even notice the money "missing" from your budget, but you can look forward to the satisfaction — excitement even — of the steady growth of your investment portfolio, as reflected in your monthly or quarterly statements.

Not all investors choose to buy mutual fund shares directly from fund companies. Some prefer to invest through full-service brokers, financial planners, or their bank or credit union (as noted in Table 8-1). Investing in this way has one significant advantage and one major disadvantage.

The advantage is the availability of investment advice and guidance. A good broker, planner, or banker should be willing to spend time analyzing your personal financial situation and be capable of offering unbiased, thoughtful suggestions concerning the best investment options for you. This individual should also have printed material to share with you that gives information about funds, investment strategies, economic forecasts, and other useful data. If you want this kind of help, consider consulting one of these financial professionals.

The disadvantage is the cost associated with this professional help. Full-service brokers and financial planners generally sell load funds rather than no-load funds.

As we explain in Chapter 6, load funds charge sales fees, often significant ones, whenever you buy shares. These fees can have a real impact on your investment profits. And, as we mention in Chapter 6, studies show that the investment performance of load funds is no better than that of no-load funds.

Therefore, the sales fees you pay buy the services of your broker, planner, or banker, but not an improvement in investment profits. For some, having an investment professional to dispense advice and guidance is priceless, but it's up to you to decide whether this advice is worth the expense for you.

Fund Supermarkets

A relatively new phenomenon in the mutual fund world are so-called *fund supermarkets.* These allow you to buy funds from several fund families for no or low transaction costs and to manage all your money in a single account. It's a convenient way to get access to thousands of mutual funds from a single source.

Fund supermarkets are still more associated with the U.S. market, as financial companies such as Charles Schwab now specialize in no-frills investment buying and selling services. Fund supermarket advisors are also paid on a fee-for-service basis in lieu of commissions.

While the Canadian fund industry has been reluctant to follow suit with fund supermarkets, there are a few signs it's reconsidering this stance. Mackenzie Financial will soon offer "institutional" shares on its funds, trimming expenses accordingly for accounts of $500,000 or more. And in December 1998, Altamira purchased no-load mutual fund dealer Mutual Fund Direct in order to sell rival load funds without commissions.

If you open an account with one of these firms, you'll be able to buy and sell shares from a wide range of fund families; switch from one fund to another with ease, even if the funds are held in different families; and receive information about all your accounts in a single statement.

Deciding When to Buy

Be careful about buying shares in a mutual fund outside a registered plan during the last quarter of the year (that is, during the months of October, November, and December). Most funds announce their dividends, capital gains, and other such profits for the year during this quarter. The problem arises when income earned by the fund over the previous 12 months is paid out (called the *distribution*) before the end of the year to investors — including you. Even if you just purchased units two weeks previous, you are now responsible for paying taxes on the entire distribution. The net effect is you receive back some of the investment money you just paid in and you have to pay tax on it.

Remember

If you are purchasing a mutual fund to hold in a tax-advantaged plan such as an RRSP, you actually have until 60 days after the tax year is over to make your purchase. Therefore, you can still be contributing up until March of the current year for last year's taxes. And with everything you contribute being deductible from your taxable income, this extra window of time should be taken advantage of as much as possible.

Dollar Cost Averaging

Dollar cost averaging is a technique whereby an investor puts a fixed amount of money into the same investment vehicle at regular intervals. For example, if Ian invests $500 a month into a mutual fund every month, he is dollar cost averaging.

Dollar cost averaging offers a number of benefits. For many investors, the habit of investing regularly is a difficult one to develop and maintain. Setting aside the same amount of money from each paycheque is a good way to develop this discipline.

Many mutual fund companies can arrange automatic deductions from your chequing or savings account, which make it even easier to invest regularly. You'll soon find that you hardly miss the money, which is going to build a steadily increasing investment nest egg.

Dollar cost averaging also increases the rate of return on your investment dollar. Here's how it works. Suppose Ian invests his $500 a month into a mutual fund whose net asset value per share varies between $20 and $40. During months when the NAV is lower, Ian's $500 will enable him to buy more shares; when the NAV is higher, he'll buy fewer shares.

The beauty of dollar cost averaging is that, over time, by investing the same amount each month, Ian will buy more shares at a relatively lower price. Therefore, his average price per share will be lower, meaning that his investment profits will be greater.

See Table 8-2 for an illustration of how this works. Over the year shown, with the NAV of Ian's Fund F varying between $20 and $40 per share, the average NAV is $30.08 per share (calculated simply by adding the average monthly NAV — $20 in January, $24 in February, and so on — and then dividing the sum by 12). But Ian has been able to buy a total of more than 208 shares for $6,000. Thus, the average per-share price Ian has actually paid is just $28.83 — more than a dollar less than the average NAV for the period.

Dollar cost averaging always works this way: By buying more shares when the price goes down, you reduce your per-share purchase price and so stretch your investing dollar.

Table 8-2:   Dollar Cost Averaging

$500 per month invested in Fund F, whose NAV varies between $20 and $40 per share. Shares purchased calculated by dividing $500 by the month's NAV.

Month	NAV	Shares Purchased
January	$20	25.00
February	24	20.83
March	28	17.86
April	22	22.73
May	26	19.23
June	34	14.71
July	40	12.50
August	37	13.51
September	33	15.15
October	30	16.67
November	32	15.63
December	35	14.29
Total shares purchased:	208.11	
Total purchase price:	$6,000.00 ($500/month × 12 months)	
Average purchase price:	$28.83	

Dollar cost averaging enables the investor to regard a decline in NAV not as a loss of value but rather an opportunity to buy more fund shares at a discount price. We strongly recommend it to all new investors — and to experienced ones who've never enjoyed its benefits.

CHAPTER 9

DEALING WITH TAXES

IN THIS CHAPTER

- Taxing dividends and capital gains
- Looking at tax-managed funds
- Cutting taxes by investing in tax-advantaged plans
- Defining allowable investments in tax-advantaged plans

As a mutual fund investor, you may find great joy in seeing that your fund is providing substantial returns. But in most cases, you have to face a downside: taxes to be paid on the profits you enjoy. Even if you're investing strictly within a tax-sheltered plan such as an RRSP, you will be taxed eventually when you withdraw your money. Income earned outside a tax-sheltered plan is subject to tax at your *marginal tax rate* (the tax rate payable on the last dollar you earn). In this chapter, we explain how mutual fund profits are taxed and some of the strategies you can use to reduce the amount you must pay to Revenue Canada.

Tax Consequences of Mutual Fund Profits

As we explain in Chapter 2, you can profit in three ways when you own a mutual fund: through any increase in the net asset value (NAV) of the fund shares; through dividends; and through capital gains. Each of these kinds of profit has a potential impact on the taxes you have to pay.

For most investors, tax considerations are not worthy of top ranking on the list of concerns that may affect decisions about buying or selling a mutual fund. Most people are wise to buy and sell mutual funds based on their changing financial goals and their perceptions of the investment markets and the overall economy rather than worrying too much about the relatively small tax consequences of their decisions.

However, if you're in a higher tax bracket (41% to 50% approximately), you may want to take the tax implications of your mutual fund investment decisions more seriously. Here are the things you need to know.

At least annually, a mutual fund must distribute to investors the interest, dividends, and capital gains that the fund's portfolio has generated over the course of the year. As we explain in Chapter 2, dividends are a portion of the profits generated by a company and shared with those who own stock in the company, and capital gains represent the difference between the price at which you purchased a security and the higher price at which you sold it — the profits.

Bond funds usually distribute the income received from their investments in the form of interest payments, sometimes on a monthly basis. Equity (stock) funds and balanced funds, which hold both stocks and bonds, may distribute dividends quarterly, annually, or semiannually.

Figure 9-1 A sample T5 Form

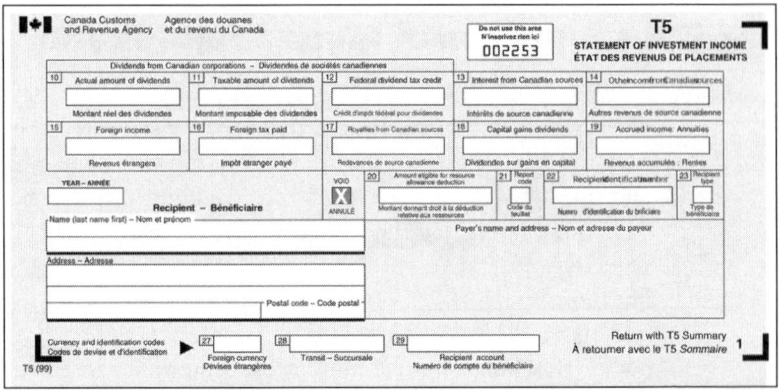
Canada Customs and Revenue Agency — Agence des douanes et du revenu du Canada

Do not use this area — N'inscrivez rien ici — 002253

T5

STATEMENT OF INVESTMENT INCOME
ÉTAT DES REVENUS DE PLACEMENTS

Dividends from Canadian corporations – Dividendes de sociétés canadiennes

10 Actual amount of dividends — Montant réel des dividendes
11 Taxable amount of dividends — Montant imposable des dividendes
12 Federal dividend tax credit — Crédit d'impôt fédéral pour dividendes
13 Interest from Canadian sources — Intérêts de source canadienne
14 Other income from Canadian sources — Autres revenus de source canadienne
15 Foreign income — Revenus étrangers
16 Foreign tax paid — Impôt étranger payé
17 Royalties from Canadian sources — Redevances de source canadienne
18 Capital gains dividends — Dividendes sur gains en capital
19 Accrued income: Annuities — Revenus accumulés : Rentes

YEAR – ANNÉE

Recipient – Bénéficiaire

VOID — ANNULÉ

20 Amount eligible for resource allowance deduction — Montant donnant droit à la déduction relative aux ressources
21 Report code — Code du feuillet
22 Recipient identification number — Numéro d'identification du bénéficiaire
23 Recipient type — Type de bénéficiaire

Name (last name first) – Nom et prénom

Payer's name and address – Nom et adresse du payeur

Address – Adresse

Postal code – Code postal

Currency and identification codes
Codes de devise et d'identification

27 Foreign currency — Devises étrangères
28 Transit – Succursale
29 Recipient account — Numéro de compte du bénéficiaire

Return with T5 Summary
À retourner avec le T5 *Sommaire* 1

T5 (99)

Reproduced with the permission of the Minister of Public Works and Government Services Canada.

Capital gains are typically distributed once a year. Around the end of the calendar year, the mutual fund company sends you a T3 or a T5 (see Figure 9-1) form detailing the taxable distributions that you received during the year. You use this information when preparing your income tax return for submission by the following April 30.

Dividends

Unless you invest your money in a tax-advantaged retirement plan (as explained later in this chapter), dividends you receive in the form of a distribution are generally treated as taxable income. However, dividends from Canadian corporations can be claimed under the *dividend tax credit,* whose net effect is to reduce the federal tax rate on Canadian corporation dividends from 26 percent to approximately 16 percent.

The dividend tax credit is calculated by grossing up your dividend by 25 percent and then multiplying the result by 13.33 percent. For example, if you earned $1,000 in dividend income, your revised dividend figure would total $1,250 ($1,000 × 125 percent). To calculate your credit, multiply your revised dividend by 13.33 percent — $1,250 × 13.33 percent = $166.62. Therefore, a total of $166.62 can be claimed when calculating your federal tax payable (*Note:* federal and provincial surtaxes are not included in calculations).

You generally have a choice (selected when you open your mutual fund account) of receiving dividend distributions in the form of a payment by cheque or reinvesting them in the purchase of additional shares of the fund. Don't fall for the myth that if you reinvest the dividends you receive, the dividends are *not* taxable.

Unfortunately, that wishful thinking is not true. Although you never actually see the dividends in the form of cash, the dividends reinvested on your behalf during the year appear on your T3 or T5 form, and Revenue Canada expects payment of all taxes due on these dividends.

If you want to avoid paying taxes on dividend income, you can opt to invest in a growth fund or a small cap fund. Such funds generally pay lower dividends than large cap funds or income funds because they invest in small companies that use their profits to finance business expansion rather than paying dividends to investors. As a result, you're likely to receive lower dividends while enjoying greater profits in the form of net asset value growth.

Warning

However, the positive tax effect of lower dividends may be spoiled if the fund's rate of turnover is unusually high. If the fund manager buys and sells stocks frequently, the fund is likely to experience greater than average capital gains, on which the individual investor must also pay taxes.

So, if you choose a fund partly to avoid heavy tax payments, make sure to check its turnover rate before investing. (Chapter 6 gives more detail on how to analyze a fund's turnover rate.)

As we previously noted and detail later in this chapter, you can also delay or avoid some tax liabilities for dividend income by putting your mutual fund investments in a tax-advantaged or sheltered plan.

Capital gains

Capital gains — profits from an increase in the value of the securities held by the mutual fund — may be either *realized* or *unrealized.* Their tax status differs accordingly, with only realized profits being eligible for taxation. Here's how it works.

Capital gains are realized when the fund manager sells stocks (or, less commonly, bonds) at a price greater than their purchase price. When stocks held by the fund increase in price but are still held, the capital gains are unrealized.

Capital gains are taxed only when they are realized. For example, suppose Sharon owns shares of Fund M, whose net asset value increases by 10 percent during the course of a year due to a 10 percent increase of the value of the stocks owned by the fund. If the fund manager sold no securities during the year, the investor would receive no realized gains in the current year — therefore, no taxes due on capital gains.

However, suppose Sharon decides to sell her shares of Fund M. (Maybe she needs to cash in her investment in order to make a down payment on a new house.) When she does so, she is realizing (literally "making real") the profits earned by the fund due to the increase in the value of the stocks it owns. These profits are now capital gains on which Sharon is obligated to pay taxes.

The longer investments are held in the portfolio in which they appreciate, the longer the tax on the capital gains is deferred. Some funds actively attempt to defer tax by minimizing the payment of distributions.

If you plan to sell your mutual fund shares, consider the tax implications of your timing. If the value of your shares has grown significantly, so that you can expect a large tax payment, consider whether you want to accelerate the transaction (making the sale by December of the current year) or to delay it (pushing it back into next January), depending on which year your income may be greater.

Realizing your profits and paying taxes on them may be less painful during a year when your income is smaller and your tax rate is therefore lower. The amount of your capital gains subject to tax can be reduced by adding any charges, such as a front-end load, to your purchase price and subtracting any expenses incurred, such as a deferred sales charge, from the sale price before calculating the amount of tax owed.

Tax-Managed Funds

Tax-managed funds are those in which tax effects are incorporated in the fund manager's decision-making process. The manager of such a fund is guided in her buying and selling decisions, in part, by considerations of how to avoid incurring excessive capital gains taxes in any given year. For example, suppose that Jane Goodbucks is the manager of Fund T, a fund that purposely attempts to reduce taxable distributions such as capital gains and dividends. Jane may be contemplating selling the fund's shares of MacMillan Bloedel, the forestry giant, because she and her research staff expect the value of MacMillan Bloedel's stock to increase at a rate of just 10 percent a year during the next several years — a little lower than Jane would like. Jane is considering replacing her MacMillan Bloedel stock with shares of Rogers Communications, the cable provider, which she expects to grow at 11 percent a year.

If Jane ignores tax effects, she is likely to sell the MacMillan Bloedel stock and buy Rogers. But because Fund T puts the tax considerations of its shareholders first, Jane considers the cost her shareholders can expect to incur for capital gains. The taxes due will depend on the amount of the gains realized, which will depend, in turn, on how long Fund T held MacMillan Bloedel and how far the stock increased during that time.

Based on these considerations, Jane may or may not decide to sell MacMillan Bloedel. Due to the effect of taxes, trading MacMillan Bloedel for Rogers may result in lower returns for investors, so holding the MacMillan Bloedel shares may be the better choice.

All fund managers buy and sell stocks during the course of a year, and any gain or loss from these transactions must be distributed to the shareholders. If a fund manager cashes in more winners than losers, shareholders are going to receive a high amount of taxable gains.

Choosing mutual funds that minimize capital gains distributions helps you defer taxes on your profits and allows your capital to compound as it would in an RRSP or other tax-advantaged plan. The more years you can compound your growth without being taxed, the greater value to you as an investor.

Canada has some tax-managed funds like those from AIC Ltd., as well as some very low turnover managers whose approach could be described as tax-managed. Canada is likely to get more of these specialty products in the next couple of years as their appeal is so strong — in the U.S., firms like Vanguard boast $3.7 billion (U.S.) in tax-managed equity funds.

Tax-advantaged mutual funds

Tax-advantaged mutual funds are funds whose investment holdings are designed to minimize the investor's tax liability. They may or may not be tax-managed, but their approach tends to be tax-efficient over time, resulting in overall lower tax payments by investors.

Index funds are the premier form of tax-advantaged investment. As we explain in Chapter 4, index funds feature a passive style of investing, in which the fund manager buys and sells stocks only as needed to ensure that the fund continues to mirror the index on which it's modeled.

Because the manager of an index fund doesn't do a lot of trading, relatively low amounts of capital gains are realized during any given year, minimizing the tax bite you must pay.

When selecting mutual funds for an account outside of a tax-advantaged plan such as an RRSP, investors often overlook tax implications. Many mutual funds and their managers actually reduce their shareholders' returns because of their tendency to produce more taxable distributions — capital gains and dividends.

By selling first all shares bought at a higher price and holding on to those bought at a lower price, a fund manager can reduce taxable distributions to investors significantly.

Tax-Advantaged Plans

If your primary investment goal is retirement, taxes need not be a major issue. Thanks to federal laws designed to encourage retirement and other types of savings, several special kinds of investment accounts are currently available that enable you to save on current taxes as you invest for retirement or for your child's postsecondary education. Any mutual fund investment can enjoy major tax benefits if it is placed in one of these tax-advantaged or sheltered plans.

Every smart investor who is putting away money for a comfortable old age owes it to himself or herself to open such an account. As you can see in Table 9-1, your money grows much faster in a tax-sheltered plan than outside.

Table 9-1: Growth of a Taxable versus a Tax-Sheltered Investment Plan

Growth on a one-time $5,000 investment, assuming an 8 percent rate of return and a combined federal and provincial tax rate of 50 percent.

Year	Outside Tax-Sheltered Plan	Inside Tax-Sheltered Plan
1	5,200	5,400
5	6,083	7,347
10	7,401	10,795
15	9,005	15,861

Year	Outside Tax-Sheltered Plan	Inside Tax-Sheltered Plan
20	10,956	23,305
25	13,329	34,242
30	16,217	50,313
35	19,730	73,927

Here's a basic guide to the kinds of tax-advantaged plans currently available in Canada.

Registered Retirement Savings Plans (RRSPs)

A Registered Retirement Savings Plan (RRSP) is an extremely tax-efficient way of saving for retirement, and in Canada, by far the largest application of mutual funds is in RRSPs. The maximum amount of your contribution to an RRSP is limited (18 percent of your previous year's income up to a maximum of $13,500), but the amount of any contribution is deducted from your taxable income, a reduction that will reward you with a tax refund. Income within an RRSP also grows untaxed.

If you are saving both inside and outside an RRSP, and have both growth and interest-paying investments, keep as much of the interest-paying holdings within your RRSP and keep the growth holdings outside where you can benefit from the lower tax rate on capital gains and dividends.

Withdrawals from an RRSP are allowed, but are fully taxed at your highest *marginal tax rate* (tax charged on the last dollar you earn). An RRSP must be terminated during the year of your 69th birthday at the latest, upon which you must cash in the plan or roll it into an RRIF, LIF, or an annuity (see the following descriptions).

Registered Retirement Income Funds (RRIFs)

A Registered Retirement Income Fund (RRIF) is a plan that allows you to hold the same investments as in your RRSP — the big difference is that instead of contributing to this plan, you must withdraw from it and pay the appropriate taxes (think of it as an RRSP in reverse). You are required to withdraw a minimum percentage of the plan's assets each year, but there is no maximum on how much you can take out. By helping gradually deplete your assets, RRIFs reduce your tax bite as only the amounts withdrawn are subject to tax.

Life Income Funds (LIFs)

These funds are created from the assets of an expired locked-in retirement account (LIRA) and are similar to an RRIF in that a minimum of assets must be withdrawn each year. However, LIFs have a cap on the maximum allowable withdrawal.

Annuities

Annuities are offered by insurance companies and banks and provide a fixed regular income for a fixed number of years in exchange for a lump sum of cash. Think of an annuity as a residential mortgage in reverse — you have given the financial institution a lump sum loan, and it pays you your money back in a regular income stream along with the interest your principal has been generating. There are two basic types of annuities — a *life* annuity provides income until your death or the death of your spouse, and a *fixed-term* annuity provides income for a set term, typically until you turn 90. Make sure you get professional advice on both of these products as they can be quite complex.

Locked-In Retirement Accounts (LIRAs)

LIRAs are like RRSPs except that contributions are "locked in" — just as early withdrawals from a pension plan aren't allowed, neither are withdrawals from a LIRA. However, you may access your LIRA within 10 years of your retirement date.

Registered Education Savings Plans (RESPs)

A Registered Education Savings Plan (RESP) is a tax-advantaged savings plan for your children's postsecondary education. Although money contributed to an RESP (limited to $4,000 per year per child to a maximum of $42,000) is not deductible for tax purposes, the government will provide a 20 percent grant on the first $2,000 in annual contributions for children up to 18 years of age to a maximum of $400 per year.

Like an RRSP, any income earned within the RESP grows untaxed. Unlike an RRSP however, there are fewer restrictions on the kinds of investments allowed in the RESP. The income from an RESP becomes taxable in your children's hands when withdrawn to finance their education, but their total income will probably be low, so little or no tax will have to be paid once educational expenses are deducted. The money you invested originally is withdrawn tax-free.

With RESPs, there are many special rules governing such matters as death, marriage breakdown, relationship requirements, grant limitations and restrictions, transfers, beneficiary changes, and of course whether your children continue their education beyond secondary school. These rules are complex — see your tax consultant and legal advisor to help you determine how these rules may affect you and what tax implications they may carry if you roll your RESP back into your RRSP.

Allowable Investments for Tax-Advantaged Plans

A minimum of 80 percent of the *book value* (the price at which the investment was purchased, as opposed to the *market value*) of the investments in the RRSP, LIRA, RRIF, or LIF must be Canadian property. To qualify as Canadian property, at least 80 percent of a mutual fund's assets must be invested in Canadian securities or assets.

Mutual funds that invest primarily outside Canada are considered "foreign property" by the federal government and cannot be registered as RRSPs. However, they can be held in a *self-directed plan* (where the choice of investments held in the plan is made by the plan holder) as part of the foreign property component, provided the total foreign property holdings do not exceed 20 percent of the plan.

CHAPTER 10
MUTUAL FUND SERVICES

IN THIS CHAPTER

- Looking into mutual fund account statements
- Seeking information and performing transactions via phone and online
- Making use of cheque-writing, automatic investment and reinvestment, and other services

When selecting a mutual fund for your investment dollars, you need to evaluate the services that the fund company offers. Some questions to ask include

- Will I have 24-hour phone access to my account?
- Can I conduct transactions via the Internet?
- How much information will be included in my account statements?
- Can I have my contributions withdrawn automatically from my account and will the income from my fund be reinvested automatically?
- Will I have the option of writing cheques against the money in my fund account?

You may be influenced to choose one fund company over another because it offers more useful services for shareholders. In this chapter, you learn about some of the services available and how to make the most of the benefits they offer.

Understanding Basic Services

The basic services that you can expect from any mutual fund company include the following:

■ Regular written reports on the performance of your investments

■ 24-hour, toll-free customer service

■ The ability to exchange money between funds in the same mutual fund family with relative ease and at little or no cost

■ The ability to make additional investments easily and quickly

■ The choice between having dividends and capital gains paid directly to you or reinvested in additional mutual fund shares

■ Cheque-writing capabilities

■ Professional advisory services

Beyond these basics, however, more and more mutual fund families are offering services that go above and beyond the call of duty. For some investors, the variety and quality of shareholder services provided is an important factor in choosing a fund or fund family in which to invest.

It's also important to keep in mind that the *quality* of basic services varies from one fund company to another. For example, account statements highlight the differences among various companies' approaches.

Account statements

Although every mutual fund provides shareholders with periodic reports on their investments, the quality, understandability, and comprehensiveness of these reports vary widely.

Most mutual fund families provide quarterly statements that let you know your current investment balance, the number of shares you own in each fund you've invested in, and your current *asset allocation* (that is, what percentage of your money is invested in which types of funds). In addition, the statement lists the transactions on your account since the last statement — new share purchases and redemptions; switching of money from one fund to another; dividend reinvestments; capital gains distributions, and so on.

If you have more than one mutual fund investment with the same family, you typically receive a combined statement showing all of your holdings rather than a separate statement for each fund. You also get a year-end statement for tax purposes, which shows balances and account activity for the entire year.

The account statements provided by most mutual fund companies provide the basics; only a few offer the luxuries. Dalbar, Inc., an independent financial research company located in Boston, has developed quality rankings for account statements from various mutual fund companies. In 1997, Dalbar looked at account statements sent out by 23 major Canadian fund managers. Of the 23, 12 were "good," one was "excellent," but 10 were deemed so unhelpful they didn't even garner a ranking. According to Dalbar's study, the top account statements, in ranking order, came from the following fund companies

- Altamira Management Ltd.
- Fidelity Investments Canada Ltd.
- GT Global Canada
- Trimark
- Talvest

Why did Dalbar rank Altamira at the top of its list? Beyond the basics, Altamira sets the standard when it comes to making tax planning easy for investors.

Altamira's statement not only lists distributions in the year to date, it also breaks them down into Canadian dividends, domestic interest, foreign income, and capital gains. Altamira also goes as far as giving investors their individual rates of return.

Among the statements receiving good rankings, were those that used features and innovations such as bold formatting for easy readibility, listing cost per unit (necessary to calculate the capital gain or loss when the fund is sold), and numerical and graphic comparisons of the cost of the investment and its current value all scored big points.

Dalbar says that most fund investors are dissatisfied with their account statements for several basic reasons:

■ The statement provides too much information. Although investors need complete data on their accounts, a fine line exists between comprehensiveness and overkill. When too much information appears on the account statement, an investor may feel overwhelmed. Fund companies are beginning to refine and improve their presentation of information by selectively eliminating less useful data and by making the data they retain easier to read through intelligent design and use of graphics. For example, many funds now show an investor's current asset allocation percentages using a pie chart rather than simply listing a set of numbers.

■ The report requires investors to translate tricky mathematical terminology. For example, some fund companies provide statistics like "average cost per share" (a number that may be useful when calculating the taxes due on mutual fund shares you've sold), but they don't describe how the number was derived. This lack of information forces you to figure it out yourself. The best account statements explain the source and meaning of every number presented.

■ The statement overestimates the investor's knowledge. Fund companies often use language that the typical investor doesn't understand. The best account statements include a brief glossary with definitions of technical terms.

When you invest in a new fund, study the first account statement carefully. Make sure that you understand every piece of data it includes. If you don't, call the fund company's information line and ask the representative to walk you through the statement, number by number.

Jot down notes as you go. And don't be afraid to ask "silly questions"! Having read this book, you know *more* than the average investor, so your questions are probably not foolish at all. After all, your money is at stake here — you deserve to know exactly what it's doing.

24-hour phone lines

You don't need to wait for a quarterly statement to get answers about your mutual fund account. Today, most fund families make information about your account as near as your telephone.

Some major fund families offer 24-hour phone lines staffed by real human beings — a welcome convenience for the millions of investors who find themselves living such busy lives that the only time they have to check their investments may be at 11:00 on a Wednesday night or 8:30 Sunday morning.

Other fund families have phone lines with live representatives only during business hours; however, they usually provide a 24-hour automated-response phone system that gives you access to your account balance and the current NAV(net asset value) of your shares and enables you to make exchanges between funds simply by using your telephone keypad. Your own coded *personal identification number* (PIN) protects your privacy, so only you can access the account.

On occasion, you may need to open a mutual fund account in a hurry. For example, you may want to make a qualifying RRSP deposit on March 1 so that you meet the annual deadline for reducing your taxes (see Chapter 9 for more on tax considerations).

Many mutual fund companies are willing to let you open an account and make a deposit by phone, even without a completed application on file, provided you submit the application soon thereafter. Call the fund of your choice, explain the situation, and provide the information the company requests, including the number of your bank account where the necessary investment money is on deposit. Then have your bank wire the money to the fund.

Online information and transactions

With the advent of the Internet, most mutual fund companies now offer the same information online that you receive in your printed account statements. In addition, you can access many other types of data and services online, which relieves much of the time and effort involved in doing research via multiple phone calls, letters, or office visits.

For example, at Trimark's Web site (`www.trimark.com`) you can find such information as

■ Historical data on how particular funds have performed

■ The largest stock or bond holdings of particular funds

■ Specific data about your accounts

Most of the things you do over the phone, you can also do online. For example, you can make investment exchanges between funds, request redemptions, and buy shares.

You can also download application forms and fund prospectuses, plus you can locate other literature on Web sites. Typically, you can access marketing brochures, articles on retirement investing, and speeches by officials at the fund company.

With each passing month, fund families are offering more and more interesting online perks. You can look forward to finding reports on the economy, glossaries of investment terms, mini-courses on investment fundamentals, and other services and features.

AGF, for example, offers an investment calculator that allows you to pick an AGF fund along with a time period and an initial investment amount — with the click of your mouse, you can find out what your returns would have been under these conditions. Many fund Web sites also feature message boards and chat rooms where you can share information and questions with other investors or with the company guru who can respond to your inquiries.

The Resource Centre at the back of this book lists some of the more useful mutual fund Web sites, but also check out your favourite fund company online — chances are, they'll also have a site worth visiting.

Automatic investment and reinvestment plans

Most fund families make it easy to set up an automatic investment plan, which is an excellent way for you to develop a consistent practice of saving. When you opt for automatic contributions to an investment account, you can also take advantage of the benefits of dollar cost averaging (refer to Chapter 8).

Ask your fund company for information about how to establish an automatic investment plan. You determine the amount that you want to designate — $100, $300, $1,000 — and the sum automatically comes out of your bank account each month and is invested in the fund of your choice. Plan to complete an application form and send in a (voided) cheque from your bank account.

You can also have the dividends and capital gains income from your funds automatically reinvested, buying you additional shares. We strongly recommend reinvesting because it allows you to enjoy the benefits of compounding, as we explain in Chapter 1.

Most fund families will allow you to have your dividend and capital gains income reinvested in a *different* fund, which can be an easy way of diversifying your portfolio.

Suppose Jacob has $5,000 invested in an index fund — a conservative, low-cost form of stock investment. Assuming his returns are substantial enough to make this transaction worthwhile, he can arrange to have the dividends and capital gains from this fund invested in the fund family's Aggressive Growth fund. As this amount gradually builds up, the growing investment gives Jacob the opportunity to participate in the profit potential of a more risky and volatile, but often lucrative, sector of the stock market — without taking any money out of his lower-risk index fund investment.

Cheque-writing

If you own shares in a fixed income fund, such as a money market fund or bond fund, you probably have the option of writing cheques against the money in your account on special cheques from the fund company. (Cheque-writing is normally *not* an option with a stock fund.)

Most funds establish a minimum amount for the cheques you write (typically $500), and you may have a small per-cheque charge. Writing a cheque can be a convenient way of redeeming shares.

When you write a cheque against a mutual fund, whether to raise some cash or to pay a bill, you are redeeming shares of your investment. Thus, you may be realizing capital gains or other profits, which subjects you to a tax liability at the end of the year. Don't forget this potential for taxable profit when the time comes to perform your tax calculations.

Retirement-related services

Many fund firms offer retirement planning services. You may be able to consult a staff member who is familiar with retirement planning issues by telephone, or you may have access to retirement planning brochures, worksheets, and other literature through the mail or online.

Typically, the retirement topics covered include the following:

■ How to calculate the amount of money you can expect to require for a comfortable and secure retirement

■ How much you need to save and invest each month in order to reach your retirement goals

■ How your asset allocation should change over time as your investment time horizon and risk tolerance change

■ The pros and cons of various kinds of tax-advantaged retirement accounts such as RRSPs, RRIFs, LIRAs, and so on.

■ Options for taking distributions from your retirement account

All Canadians who have worked either for a company or for themselves are eligible for the Canadian Pension Plan (CPP) or the Quebec Pension Plan (QPP). These plans play a role in retirement planning for most Canadians. As an employee, both you and your employer contribute equally to the CPP (or QPP in Quebec), and if you're self-employed, you pay both parts of the contribution yourself.

Although the CPP is in trouble because it's getting to the point where more people will be taking money out of the system than contributing to it, there should still be some form of plan in place when you retire, no matter how old you are today.

The amount of your monthly CPP/QPP benefits in retirement depends on the contributions made on your behalf during your work years. To find out exactly how much you can expect, contact Health and Welfare Canada (Quebec residents should contact the QPP at 1-800-463-5185) or call the Income Securities Program information service at 1-800-277-9914.

When you receive more precise information, you can develop some perspective on your expected monthly CPP/QPP payments — and how much more retirement income you'll need to provide through your own savings and investments.

Advisory services

Many mutual fund investors are self-directed: They educate themselves through books like this one, personal finance magazines and TV programs, and brochures and prospectuses offered by the fund companies. Then they make their fund selections and monitor the growth of their investments in order to make sure that they perform as expected. One reason for the popularity of mutual funds is that they lend themselves to just this kind of do-it-yourself investing.

However, if you feel that you would benefit by getting some professional financial help, some of the most qualified advisors are the ones with the Certified Financial Planner (CFP) designation after their names.

While almost anyone (outside of Quebec) is still free to use the term "financial planner" regardless of their qualifications, the CFP designation issued by the Financial Planners Standards Council indicates that your advisor is completely capable of covering everything from asset allocation approaches to investment strategies. In addition, only financial planners who are registered with the Investment Dealers Association can make recommendations as to investments. These registrants are usually employed by a full-service brokerage company and are usually called investment advisors or investment representatives.

Be sure you understand exactly how your advisor derives her compensation. An advisor who receives a fee directly from you for her services — either in the form of a straight payment or as a percentage of the assets you invest — is likely to give relatively unbiased advice (how knowledgeable or helpful this guidance proves to be is another matter).

On the other hand, advisors who receive all or part of their payments in the form of sales commissions may recommend that you buy the investment products from which they stand to benefit personally. A stockbroker may urge you to invest in stocks; an insurance agent may direct you toward insurance company products such as annuities. Before you buy into any sales pitch, carefully consider the source and what the advisor has to gain from your investment.

CLIFFSNOTES REVIEW

Use this CliffsNotes Review to practise what you've learned in this book and to build your confidence as you begin your adventures in mutual funds investing. After you work through the review questions, the problem-solving exercises, and the thought-provoking practice projects, you'll be well on your way to achieving your goal of becoming a savvy mutual funds investor!

Q&A

1. Owning a mutual fund provides diversification for your investment funds because a mutual fund

   a. Is guaranteed by an agency of the federal government

   b. Owns many different stocks or bonds

   c. Is managed by a highly educated money manager

2. When the price of stocks owned by a mutual fund increases, the investors in the fund benefit from

   a. An increase in the fund's net asset value (NAV)

   b. The payment of dividends

   c. Savings on income taxes

3. Generally, the most conservative and least risky of the following three fund types is the

   a. Emerging market equity fund

   b. High-yield bond fund

   c. Money market fund

4. International equity funds are more risky than Canadian-only equity funds partly because of

   a. High rates of Canadian taxation on foreign investments

   b. The danger of changes in currency exchange rates

   c. The low dividends paid by foreign companies

5. A government bond fund is an appropriate investment choice for someone most concerned with

   a. Reducing tax payments

   b. The security of the investment

   c. Rapid growth in the value of the investment

6. The main advantage of holding mutual funds inside of an RRSP is

   a. They can grow and compound tax-free

   b. You can make a withdrawal anytime without facing a tax penalty

   c. There is no limit on how much foreign content you can hold

7. Generally, you should consider buying shares of a closed-end mutual fund only when they are priced _____.

8. Regular dividends are most likely to be paid by

   a. A young, quickly growing company

   b. An old, established, and successful company

   c. A company that is struggling to survive financially

9. The easiest way to determine the annual cost of investing in a particular fund is to look in the prospectus for the fund's

_____.

10. A balanced fund is one that invests in both

   a. Canadian and foreign companies

   b. Corporate and government bonds

   c. Stocks and bonds

Answers: (1) b. (2) a. (3) c. (4) b. (5) b. (6) a. (7) At a discount to the net asset value (NAV). (8) b. (9) Management expense ratio (MER). (10) c.

Scenarios

1. You are 30 years old, and you are saving for retirement by investing in a mid cap growth fund. One day you receive a quarterly statement from the fund showing that, during the past three months, the value of the investments in the fund has fallen by 10 percent. You should _____
_____.

2. Based on your reading and on personal business experience, you've become convinced that the health care industry is likely to experience major growth in sales and profits in the next 20 years. To enjoy the benefits of this growth through mutual fund investments, you should consider investing in _____
_____.

3. You hold a number of equity funds outside of your RRSP and are getting heavily taxed on the dividends and capital gains you're realizing. One way to cut down on your taxes is to_____
_____.

Answers: (1) Stay invested; your investment time frame is a long one, which means that the fund has plenty of time to recover its value and resume steady growth. (2) A specialty or sector fund that specializes in the health care industry. (3) Take advantage of the dividend tax credit which effectively reduces the tax levied on dividends of Canadian corporations from 26 percent to approximately 16 percent.

Consider This

■ Did you know that most mutual fund families can make it easy for you to invest a fixed amount every month through an automatic deduction from your chequing account? It's a great way to make your savings grow painlessly with no need for self-discipline on your part. (See Chapter 8 for more information about buying funds directly from fund management companies.)

■ Did you know that savings invested in an RRSP or other type of tax-deferred account grow faster than in an ordinary investment account? Almost everyone is eligible to participate in one or more of these special plans. (See Chapter 9 for more information on how to save on taxes as your retirement savings grow.)

■ Did you know that index funds, which invest in all the stocks that are part of a particular stock market index, regularly outperform other types of mutual funds, while running up lower management fees? Growing numbers of investors are making index funds their favourite way to invest. (See Chapter 4 for more information on index funds and how they work.)

Practice Projects

1. Read the coverage of mutual funds in a recent issue of a financial magazine or newspaper. Find the names and phone numbers of three mutual funds that interest you and request a copy of the prospectus for each (as explained in Chapter 7). Read the prospectuses and decide whether one of these funds might make a sound investment for you.

2. Boot up your computer and jump online to view the information offered on various funds at sites such as Portfolio Analytics (www.pal.com), Globefund (www.globefund.com) and The Fund Library (www.fundlibrary.com). Compare the information presented in the three reports. Which do you find most understandable? Most interesting? Most helpful? (See Chapter 7 for more information on using this and other types of mutual fund information and analysis.)

3. List your three most important short-term financial goals and your three most important long-term financial goals (as we explain in Chapter 1). For each goal, estimate the amount of money you'll need to reach the goal and the number of months or years it will take to reach the goal. Then decide how much money you can set aside each month to invest in mutual funds in pursuit of these goals.

CLIFFSNOTES RESOURCE CENTRE

The learning has just begun! CliffsNotes Resource Centre shares information on outstanding print and online sources of additional information about mutual funds. The organizations, publications, and other sources listed here are popular, well respected, authoritative voices in the financial industry, and we believe you can gain valuable insight from checking out what they have to offer. Look for these terrific resources at your favourite bookstore and on the Internet. When you're online, make your first stop www.cliffnotes.com, where you'll find more incredibly useful information on mutual funds.

Books

This CliffsNotes book is one of many great books on mutual funds and investment topics published by IDG Books Worldwide, Inc. So if you want some great next-step books, check out these other publications.

CliffsNotes Investing for the First Time for Canadians, by Marguerite Pigeon and Tracey Longo, introduces you to commonly available investment options and invites you to create a plan with your newfound knowledge of investing. CDG Books Canada, $8.99.

Investing For Canadians For Dummies, by Eric Tyson and Tony Martin, is the perfect book for people looking to develop an investment strategy. CDG Books Canada, $27.99.

Investing Online For Canadians For Dummies, by Andrew Dagys and Kathleen Sindell, is an ideal guide to a vast array of Internet investment tools, links, and resources. CDG Books Canada, $27.99.

Personal Finance For Dummies For Canadians, 2nd Edition, by Eric Tyson and Tony Martin, is a rich money management resource for anyone who wants to enjoy the rewards of smart money management. IDG Books, $26.99.

Gordon Pape's 2000 Buyer's Guide to RRSPs, by Gordon Pape, rates the best mutual funds to hold for your RRSP and RRIF, and provides tips on how to profit from foreign content. Prentice Hall Canada, $19.95.

Chand's World of Mutual Funds, by Ranga Chand, tracks and rates the performance of more than 1,500 Canadian and international funds. Also offers valuable insights and contact information for every mutual fund company. Stoddart Publishing, $22.95.

It's easy to find books published and distributed by CDG Books Canada, Inc. including all of the popular lines from IDG Books Worldwide, Inc. You can find them in your favourite bookstores near you and on the Internet. There are four Web sites that you can use to read about our entire line of books:

- www.cdgbooks.com
- www.cliffnotes.com
- www.dummies.com
- www.idgbooks.com

Internet

Check out these Web sites for more information on mutual funds and other investment topics:

Globefund.com, www.globefund.com is one of Canada's shining stars for all kinds of mutual fund investment information. This site offers historical performance data, fund rankings, online investing, and a weekly fund profile feature.

Portfolio Analytics, www.pal.com features impressive and in-depth fund profile information along with an archive of feature reports, polls, news, and analysis.

Canoe Money, www.canoe.com boasts daily, weekly, and monthly mutual fund listings all combined in one search engine. One impressive feature on this site is a tool that allows comparison of current and recent pricing of any fund to similar funds for the same periods.

The Fund Counsel, www.fundcounsel.com is chock-full of mutual fund information based on the Fund Counsel's newsletter and also features manager profiles, polls, forums, and investment games.

The Fund Library, www.fundlibrary.com contains over 10,000 pages of information that cover every mutual fund available in Canada. Create your own list of funds to track and chart or join their online discussion group.

Investor Learning Centre of Canada, www.investor-learning.ca is a low-key, user-friendly site that has a helpful set of financial and mutual fund links of definite interest to Canadian investors.

Greenpage$, http://magi.com/~mftrackr/ is a thorough list of links for just about every fund Canadian mutual fund family.

Magazines & Newspapers

Most financial magazines and newspapers provide regular coverage of mutual funds. The following publications generally are considered authoritative and reliable.

Canadian MoneySaver is a monthly magazine that features practical advice from money experts on a variety of financial and investment topics. $2.95/issue.

IE: Money is a magazine published six times per year and features clear and comprehensive "how to" strategies on building and protecting your financial future. This magazine also features an annual issue dedicated to mutual funds. $3.95/issue.

Canadian Business publishes 21 issues per year covering everything from business to travel to technology, with plenty of attitude to spare. Also runs a special issue on mutual funds. $3.95/issue.

Mutual Fund Review is a quarterly magazine featuring opinions and articles from such writers as Levi Folk and Garth Turner. This magazine focuses on issues that affect Canadian investors. $4.25/issue.

Report on Business is a monthly magazine that covers a variety of financial and investment categories including mutual funds. Free with *Globe and Mail* subscription.

You can find these publications at your neighbourhood bookstore. Visit the Web sites (or your local library) for an overview of the style and contents of each periodical.

Send Us Your Favourite Tips

In your quest for learning, have you ever experienced that sublime moment when you figure out a trick that saves time or trouble? Perhaps you realized you were taking ten steps to accomplish something that could have taken two. Or you've found a little-known workaround that gets great results. If you've discovered a useful tip that helped you make decisions about mutual funds more effectively, and you'd like to share it, CliffsNotes would love to hear from you. Go to our Web site at www.cliffsnotes.com and click the Talk to Us button. If we select your tip, we may publish it as part of CliffsNotes Daily, our exciting free e-mail newsletter. To find out more, or to subscribe to a newsletter, go to www.cliffnotes.com on the Web.

INDEX

A

account statements, 95, 96-99
account
  opening, 100
  setting up fund account, 77
active investing, 40
administrative costs, 60, 61-62, 64
administrative fee, 62
advisor's fee, 105
advisory services, 104-105
AGF, 21, 22, 101
aggressive growth funds, 44-45, 67
AIC Ltd., 89
Alberta Stock Exchange (ASE), 39
Altamira Management Ltd., 58, 79, 97, 98
annual operating expenses, 59-65
annualized returns, 68
annuities, 92
asset allocation, 97
automatic deductions
  from account, 60
  from paycheque, 81
automatic investment plans, 6, 29, 30, 78, 101-102
automatically withdrawn contributions, 95
average cost per share, 98

B

back-end load, 57-58
balanced funds, 54, 67, 84
banks, interest rates, 51
BCE Inc., 42
bear market, 32, 38
BellCharts, 69
blue chip stocks, 42
Bombardier, 18
bond funds, 36, 37, 38, 50, 61, 67, 84, 102
bonds, 16, 18
  corporate, 38, 52-53
  government, 38, 52, 67
  high yield, 52-53
  junk, 52-53

sale of, 19
  short term, 50, 51
  trading of, 19
broker, 18
  full service, 57, 78
budget, maintaining, 11
bull markets, 32

C

Canada Deposit Insurance Corporation (CDIC), 33, 51
Canada Mortgage and Housing Corporation (CMHC), 53
Canada Pension Plan (CPP), 2, 104
Canadian Bond Rating Service, 52
Canadian Business, 68
Canadian Moneysaver, 68
Canoe Money, 112
capital gains, 20, 23-24, 23-24, 34, 40, 43, 77, 78, 80, 83, 84, 85, 91, 102, 103
  and tax status, 86-87
  minimizing, 89
  realized, 86
  unrealized, 86
capital, 50
cash equivalent, 51
cash flow, increasing, 12
Certified Financial Planner (CFP), 105
Charles Schwab, 79
cheque-writing, 102-103
CliffsNotes Daily, 4
CliffsNotes Resource Centre, 3, 68, 70, 101, 110-113
CliffsNotes Web site, 4
closed-end funds
  selling at discount, 25
  selling at premium, 25
commissions, 56, 57, 59, 63, 64
common shares, 53
compounding, 6, 13-15, 78, 102
conservative investment, 50
control
  lack of, 31
  over investments, 31
corporate bond funds, 38, 52-53
cost, investing in funds, 29
credit card, reducing debt, 12-13
currency risk, 46, 47, 48
currency values, in emerging market funds, 48

Notes

COMING SOON FROM CLIFFSNOTES

Online Shopping

HTML

Choosing a PC

Beginning Programming

Careers

Windows 98 Home Networking

eBay Online Auctions

PC Upgrade and Repair

Business

Microsoft Word 2000

Microsoft PowerPoint 2000

Finance

Microsoft Outlook 2000

Digital Photography

Palm Computing

Investing

Windows 2000

Online Research

CDG
BOOKS
CANADA

COMING SOON FROM CLIFFSNOTES
Buying and Selling on eBay

Have you ever experienced the thrill of finding an incredible bargain at a specialty store or been amazed at what people are willing to pay for things that you might toss in the garbage? If so, then you'll want to learn about eBay — the hottest auction site on the Internet. And CliffsNotes *Buying and Selling on eBay* is the shortest distance to eBay proficiency. You'll learn how to:

■ Find what you're looking for, from antique toys to classic cars

■ Watch the auctions strategically and place bids at the right time

■ Sell items online at the eBay site

■ Make the items you sell attractive to prospective bidders

■ Protect yourself from fraud

Here's an example of how the step-by-step CliffsNotes learning process simplifies placing a bid at eBay:

1. Scroll to the Web page form that is located at the bottom of the page on which the auction item itself is presented.

2. Enter your registered eBay username and password and enter the amount you want to bid. A Web page appears that lets you review your bid before you actually submit it to eBay. After you're satisfied with your bid, click the Place Bid button.

3. Click the Back button on your browser until you return to the auction listing page. Then choose View⇨Reload (Netscape Navigator) or View⇨Refresh (Microsoft Internet Explorer) to reload the Web page information. Your new high bid appears on the Web page, and your name appears as the high bidder.